S0-AUQ-043

THE ART OF MAKING REAL SOUPS

A Delicious Collection of Recipes
from Round the World

The Art of Making
REAL SOUPS
A Delicious Collection of Recipes from Round the World

BY MARIAN TRACY

With Drawings by Grambs Miller

Garden City, New York

DOUBLEDAY & COMPANY, INC.

Printed in the United States of America

For Bergen and Jean Evans

Contents

Recipes for items marked with an asterisk (*) can be located by consulting the Index.

Introduction

Soup is one of the most ancient dishes in the world, as much the very essence of life as bread and wine. As Bishop Latour says in Willa Cather's *Death Comes for the Archbishop,* after tasting one of Father Vaillant's soups, "A soup like this is not the work of one man. It is the result of a constantly refined tradition. There are nearly a thousand years of history in this soup." That particular soup of Father Vaillant's was a rich, dark and suave onion soup; the combination of ingredients was not quite that old. Possibly Bishop Latour was thinking back to the first man who grew an onion, the first one who put meat and water in a pot over heat to make a broth and so on.

Soup is one of the most comforting dishes to make, pleasurable in its aroma, also in the companionable sound of its quiet burbling, and in its infinite variety. On a long gray day when all is not right with my world, a pot of soup simmering on the stove in an undemanding way soothes and heartens me. In the making it nourishes my spirits as much as it nourishes and sustains me physically later on.

There is a folk tale that appears in many versions in many lands. A hungry soldier, on his way home from war, asks an old woman for a meal at a farmhouse but she tells him that she has no food. Resourceful and undaunted, he shows her a stone that he claims is a magic one that makes soups. He offers to demonstrate if she will lend him a kettle and let him make a fire. She does and he fills the kettle with water, adds the stone and waits until the water comes to a boil. Then he tastes it, makes approving sounds but says that it needs a little salt. The old woman, who has been watching with wonder, gets the salt, and he adds it to the kettle. Tasting again, he says that an onion would improve the flavor. She gets an onion and it is added to the pot, then a carrot when he suggests that. Then he muses about how much better the soup would be with just a little cabbage, which the old woman also contributes. Soon there is a fine soup simmering in the kettle which they eat together cozily. When he leaves to go on his way, she begs for the magic soup stone. In some versions, he sells it to her.

To make soup, even in a folk tale, the soldier needed more than a stone, and in real life one needs good ingredients, although not necessarily expensive ones. It is also a good idea to have some skill, intelligence and the good sense to leave well enough alone—to omit superfluities. Given a cook of good instincts and a gay imagination, the same soup never need be repeated from one year's end to the next.

In these days with supermarkets everywhere in the land, few people *have* a butcher, much less one to save them free soupbones as is said to have happened in the good old days (always before you came along). However, an interested and determined bone collector can find some from time to time in the meat sections of the supermarket, tidily packaged and labeled. It is best to buy lots and squirrel them away in the freezing unit of the refrigerator or in the freezer against the time when you will want them. A soup-making day or mood can come upon one suddenly, and if a suitable number of ingredients are on hand, one can relax and enjoy it.

Even in a city apartment it is possible to keep some bones in the freezer, onions, carrots, lemons, celery, potatoes and herbs elsewhere. There should also be canned tomatoes, beef bouillon (homemade, canned or a beef-stock base), chicken (ditto), barley, all kinds of beans (canned or dried) rice and pasta in lots of the small, charming shapes (wagon wheels, butterflies, seashells, etc.) and the pretty layered packages of legumes, seasonings, barley and so on called minestrone mix. Always have a few frozen green vegetables to be added to the soup in the last minutes of cooking as a fresh, crisp accent.

A soup maker has a happy feeling when there is a ham bone in the refrigerator or the carcass of a roast chicken, duck or turkey, all blessed by-products, as are compatible cooked vegetables and cooked meats. On the other hand, a soup pot is not a disposal. Some things do not taste well together, so select with caution, with imagination and taste. Discard the mediocre and unharmonious.

Sometimes a soup is all right but somehow tastes a little flat. When that occurs, try one or two of these but not all to make the flavor sparkle, as it were: a lemon, sliced thin; a few tomatoes or tomato paste or purée; sour salt (just a few crystals); a chopped onion sautéed or raw; a dash of an herb powdered first in the palm of the hand; some chopped fresh dill (one of the best soup herbs with an intoxicating flavor *and* fragrance); or use a little grated cheese or a dollop of sour cream or one of the other garnishes mentioned in Chapter 13.

After a soup has been made and served, refrigerate or freeze any that remains. Those dreamy instructions in old books about keeping the soup on the back of the stove and reheating once a day do not make sense these days. It is true that houses used to be kept colder, but either people were more immune to the sneaky little bacilli in spoiled food or else they blamed it on something else. Soups that are left out will sometimes ferment overnight with a furious boiling sound or if left longer grow a rich and repulsive-looking fungus. Once my brother was staying with me temporarily, and I left him a large pot of oxtail soup to sustain him while I was gone. He didn't bother with it before he, too, left. When we both came back, the bones were covered with a long-haired white mold. I let him clean things up after what I *think* was an amicable discussion. Soup also gets a tired taste and look after too much reheating, so it is best to freeze it in small containers and use what is needed each time, adding one of the flavor sparklers described above, a package of frozen green vegetable, a dash of wine, etc. Freezing is especially fine for a household of one or two people because then it is possible to have the pleasure of making and eating soup without the boredom of eating it continuously, night after night, until it is gone. Also, it is a nice feeling to have some stashed away in the freezer on a night when it seems a bore to cook for one.

Some special equipment is needed but not much. A two- or three-gallon pot is necessary for the bulky stages of making stock or minestrone or other large soups. It can be of inexpensive enamelware, a heavy cast aluminum, stainless steel, copper or what you will. A cast-iron Dutch oven will do for some soups but will turn those with tomatoes an undecorative dark color, but otherwise is all right. If the soup pot has a long handle, it can hang on the wall out of the way and can be used to steam lobsters or crabs or mussels, cook pasta and other foods which need a large pan. A collander and a food mill or an electric blender are needed, to drain and purée soups. It is assumed that most kitchens have sharp knives for chopping, long wooden spoons for stirring, a bulb baster for removing fat from the top of a soup when there is not time to chill it and plastic containers for freezers.

A soup tureen is expensive and not really essential; the soup *can* be served in the kitchen, but a tureen is almost always one of the most beautiful and hospitable-looking of the large serving pieces and can be used for flowers in between times. People who buy china in sets usually have something labeled a soup bowl, but that is not for me. I love things that harmonize but do not match and have many different kinds of bowls in many shapes, colors and textures and am easily beguiled by a new shape that is especially beautiful, that seems perfect for a special soup. Admittedly, this is not normal, and when I move, china packers glare at me. Delicate soups look beautiful in thin rice bowls or in seashells of interesting shapes. Clear glass bowls make cold soups look even cooler. On the other hand, large bulky soups, the meal-in-themselves kind need bowls of an ample size, as do most seafood soups. They need not be costly, nor do all sizes have to be bought at the same time.

Soup is a hospitable dish and adaptable to the complexities of present-day living when children come and go on incompatible schedules, to lazy Sunday nights when the hour for eating depends upon the mood, to the currently chic and relaxed kind of entertaining when people come for cocktails and stay for soup and leisurely conversation.

In this book, quite naturally, the suggested menus have been planned to complement the soups and may be mixed and matched at will or totally disregarded. Please consult your favorite cookbook for the recipes.

Cooking times herein given are approximate. Even in these days of controlled temperatures, each stove has a metabolism of its own, and the age and tenderness of meat and vegetables vary. Most soups except for a few cream soups discussed elsewhere accommodate to varying heats, although a low or medium is usually the best in most cases.

For the other cookbooks that I have compiled, there have usually been a definite few people who have given me some kind of help, but for this, there have been an infinite many: all those who have fed me, my mind and my enthusiasms for a long time. This cookbook, more than any of my others, is a part of the ways I have lived, eaten, cooked, and felt and all the books I have read. The idea of the book may have been dormant since the time Nino and I bought, in the first lean, brief but happy years of our marriage, a beautiful antique Russian copper soup pot that holds two gallons which has been very much part of every kitchen I have had since then.

I

Celestial Beginnings

These are the delicate and decorative and flavorful preamble to a meal, which suggest and complement the meal to come. They tempt the eye as well as the nose and palate.

CELESTIAL SOUP WITH ROYAL CUSTARD

It's celestially simple if not exactly frugal.

1 can clear turtle soup
1 can clear beef bouillon
½ teaspoon curry powder
Grated peel of ½ lemon
Royal custard, cut into small shapes*

Simmer the turtle soup and bouillon, stirring to blend. Add the curry powder and grated lemon peel. Add the custard shapes. Serve very hot in bouillon cups with sandwiches made of very thin slices of bread, fresh unsalted butter and thin cucumber slices. *Serves 4.*

Royal Custard

1 whole egg
2 egg yolks
½ cup consommé or heavy cream
Salt and freshly ground black pepper

Preheat oven to 300°. Beat the egg and egg yolks until light. Stir in the cream. Season with salt and pepper and pour mixture into a shallow buttered pan. Set the pan in a larger pan with about an inch of hot water. Bake until firm—about twenty minutes. Cool and chill. Cut into small, fancy shapes with a knife or small vegetable cutters. Use as a garnish for soup.

MENU:

CELESTIAL SOUP WITH ROYAL CUSTARD
THIN CUCUMBER SANDWICHES AND UNSALTED BUTTER
VEAL PICCATA
NOODLES
SPINACH SALAD
BLACK BING CHERRIES WITH THIN CUSTARD SAUCE

JULIENNE SOUP WITH POLPETTE

Somehow a soup with the vegetables cut into slender matchstick pieces, julienne fashion, and barely cooked is very elegant. Add some tiny meatballs or polpette, as the Italians call them, for substance and flavor.

Tiny Meatballs

½ pound chopped beef
1 egg
Salt and pepper

Julienne Soup

4 cups beef bouillon
1 turnip, cut julienne
3 carrots, cut julienne
1 bunch spring onions, cut julienne
2 branches celery, cut julienne
3 medium beets, cut julienne
1 bunch parsley, finely chopped
½ teaspoon thyme
Salt and pepper

Mix the chopped beef with the egg and seasoning and make into tiny balls about the size of a radish. Heat the beef bouillon, add the julienne vegetables, cook for about 15 minutes. Add the meatballs and simmer for 3 to 5 minutes. Serve with 4 or 5 meatballs in each bowl. *Serves 4 or 5.*

MENU:

JULIENNE SOUP WITH POLPETTE
STEAK WITH BROILED MUSHROOM CAPS
MASHED POTATOES
STRAWBERRIES
CHOCOLATE LEAVES

JELLIED MUSHROOM SOUP

This could be made out of many fascinating, variously flavored and variously colored wild mushrooms, but it is best to stick with the fresh mushrooms available in markets unless you are an experienced mycologist.

½ pound fresh mushrooms
6 cups chicken broth
¼ cup Madeira wine
Sour cream
Pinch of tarragon
Few grains nutmeg

Put the mushrooms in a blender with a cup of chicken broth and chop thoroughly or put through a meat grinder. Put the chopped mushrooms in a pot with the chicken broth and bring to a rolling boil. Remove from the fire, cover and let steep until lukewarm. Strain through cheesecloth into a saucepan and boil down until reduced to about 4 cups. Check the seasoning, add salt and pepper now if there was not enough seasoning in the broth. Cool and then chill in the refrigerator for at least 4 hours. When ready to serve, stir in the Madeira and serve in chilled cups. Garnish each with a tablespoon of sour cream sprinkled with tarragon and nutmeg. *Serves 4.*

MENU:

JELLIED MUSHROOM SOUP
BEEF STROGANOFF
KASHA
WATERCRESS AND LEAF LETTUCE SALAD WITH LEMON DRESSING
LEMON SOUFFLÉ

CAPPELLETTI ALLA ROMAGNOLA

This is a chicken and cheese version of ravioli and won ton. Unlike ravioli, but like won ton, it is cooked and served in broth. The cappelletti are heavy and sink to the bottom at first. When they float to the top they are done.

The Stuffing

1 whole chicken breast, sautéed in butter and chopped
⅔ cup ricotta cheese
2 tablespoons freshly grated Parmesan cheese
2 egg yolks
1 egg white
⅛ teaspoon nutmeg
⅛ teaspoon grated lemon peel
Salt and pepper to taste

The Dough

2 cups sifted flour
2 eggs
¼ cup water
½ teaspoon salt

The Soup

2½ quarts chicken broth, homemade or canned

Mix all the ingredients for the stuffing into a smooth paste. Place in the refrigerator until ready to use. Place the flour on a board. Make a depression in the center and place the eggs, water and salt in it. With a fork gradually beat the eggs and water with flour until about half of the flour is used up. Add the remaining flour by hand and knead into a smooth firm paste. If the dough is too soft, add a little flour. Knead for 10 minutes. Cut the dough in half and roll out on floured board into 2 very thin round sheets. With a round cookie cutter about 2¼ or 2½ inches in diameter, cut both sheets of dough, wasting as little dough as possible. Place ¼ teaspoon of stuffing in the center of each circle of dough. Dampen the edge of the circle facing you with a finger dipped in water. Fold the disk, closing in stuffing, by pressing with fingertips. Bring the two corners together and, if necessary, dampen one corner lightly with a wet finger to make it stick. Repeat this operation until all ingredients are used (makes about 2 dozen caps). Bring the broth to the boiling point, add the cappelletti and cook 15 to 20 minutes. It is quite possible that a few tablespoons of stuffing will be left over, depending on the thickness of the dough sheets. If desired, this can be used as a spread for canapés. The cappelletti can be made in advance and kept in the refrigerator between sheets of waxed paper, or frozen, until ready to cook. This soup is usually served by Italians during the Christmas holidays. *Serves 8 to 10.*

MENU:

CAPPELLETTI ALLA ROMAGNOLA
SALAD NIÇOISE
BLUEBERRY CHEESECAKE

DRIED MUSHROOM BROTH WITH SNOW PEAS

Dried mushrooms, which sound frighteningly expensive when priced by the pound for the first time, are not really expensive. They are so light in weight that a few ounces go a long way. They have much more flavor than the canned ones.

⅓ cup dried mushrooms
4 cups homemade or canned chicken broth
½ teaspoon grated lemon peel
4 spring onions, with tops and bottoms, chopped
¼ cup French dry vermouth
½ package frozen Chinese snow peas or 1 cup fresh Chinese snow peas
Salt, if necessary

Soak the mushrooms for an hour or more in 1 or 2 cups of chicken broth. When soft, cut them in quarters. Cook in the chicken broth with the lemon peel, spring onions, and vermouth over medium heat for about 20 minutes; then add the peas and cook until pea pods are barely tender but crisp. Check the seasoning; some chicken broth has enough. Add salt if necessary. *Serves 4 to 6.*

MENU:

DRIED MUSHROOM BROTH WITH SNOW PEAS
DELMONICO STEAKS CREAMED SPINACH
BROILED TOMATO HALVES PEARS AND CHEESE

HAM AND CELERY SOUP

A French soup with a delicate and savory flavor and a crisp contrast of texture not unlike some of the Oriental combinations.

2 onions, chopped
1 tablespoon flour
3 tablespoons butter
6 cups beef stock
⅓ cup julienne pieces of ham
4 ribs celery, cut in thin slices

Sprinkle the onions with flour. Cook in the butter over medium heat for a few minutes until they are yellow and limp but not brown. Add the stock and ham. Simmer for 15 to 20 minutes, or longer if you wish. This will wait amiably. Just before serving, add the cold raw celery. *Serves 4.*

MENU:

HAM AND CELERY SOUP
DANISH OPEN-FACED SANDWICHES
BLUEBERRIES AND CREAM

DUCK SOUP

Despite the phrase "easy as duck soup," there are few recipes for it around. Yet with all the Long Island ducklings on the market there must be some carcasses going to waste. Naturally, if the carcass you have is either chicken or turkey this will work equally well. It is best, of course, if there is some meat left over or some on the bones.

1 carcass duck, chicken or turkey
1 onion, quartered
1 cup chopped celery with the leaves
1 carrot, quartered
¼ cup chopped parsley
½ teaspoon mixed pickling spice
Bouquet garni:
½ bay leaf
3 sprigs chervil
3 sprigs parsley
Salt
1 cup rice and wild rice mixture
1 package frozen artichoke hearts, quartered
⅓ cup French dry vermouth
½ cup cold melon balls

Break the carcass into pieces and put in a pot with 4 to 6 cups of water. The amount will depend on how large the carcass is or how many carcasses you have. Add the onion, celery, carrot, parsley, pickling spice and bouquet garni. Simmer for about 1½ hours; then strain the soup and chill it. Remove the fat and put the soup in another pan with the mixed rice, artichoke hearts and vermouth. Add enough liquid, either chicken cubes in some water or plain water, to make a little over a quart and a pint of liquid. Simmer until the rice and artichoke hearts are tender. Salt and serve with a few cold melon balls in each bowl. *Serves 4 to 6.*

MENU:

DUCK SOUP
CLAM FRITTERS
JANSSON'S TEMPTATION (scalloped potatoes with anchovies)
FRESH PEACHES AND CREAM

DRIED MUSHROOM SOUP II

If fresh mushrooms are not available, dried ones, which can be kept on hand, are preferable to the canned ones for flavor. They seem to have the distilled essence of mushrooms within them.

⅓ cup dried mushrooms, soaked in a little water
1 clove garlic, minced
1 tomato, quartered
4 cups chicken or beef broth
½ cup heavy cream
1 tablespoon freshly grated Parmesan cheese
1 tablespoon finely chopped parsley

Put the mushrooms, which have been soaked and drained, with the garlic and tomato in the broth. Simmer very gently for about an hour until the mushrooms are completely soft. Strain the soup and discard the mushrooms. Stir in the cream, cheese and parsley just before serving. *Serves 4.*

MENU:
DRIED MUSHROOM SOUP
HOT BISCUITS
SALMON PUDDING
CUCUMBER AND WATERCRESS SALAD
ORANGE CRUMB PIE

BLACK WALNUT SOUP

This is not a soup to serve to the unwary. Black walnuts are very much an acquired taste. People have to get used to the rather gamy flavor. Once they do, an exciting new taste world opens up.

2 tablespoons fat
4 tablespoons flour
Salt
Cayenne pepper
4½ cups strong chicken or beef broth
1 bay leaf
½ cup chopped black walnuts
¾ cup thin cream
2 tablespoons sour cream
1 pinch freshly chopped or dried marjoram
⅓ cup sour red cherries, drained (nice but not obligatory)

Melt the fat in a pan. Stir in the flour, salt and pepper. Pour in the broth and stir over the fire until the soup comes to a boil. Add the bay leaf and walnuts and simmer for 15 minutes. Add the cream, sour cream and marjoram and simmer for 2 minutes. Remove the bay leaf, add cherries and serve. *Serves 6.*

MENU:
BLACK WALNUT SOUP CLAM PIE
FRESH RASPBERRIES

ONION SOUP

French onion soup makes people dream of Paris and of eating the soup with wall-to-wall cheese toast in Les Halles at dawn. According to the distinguished collaboration called *Mastering the Art of French Cooking,* it should be cooked for 3 hours or more. Equally distinguished authorities such as Louis Diat and Joseph Donon say about 15 minutes. This is the short method.

2 cups sliced onion
½ cup (1 stick) butter
1½ quarts beef stock or bouillon
Salt
Freshly ground black pepper
4 thick slices French bread, toasted
½ cup grated Parmesan cheese

Sauté the onions in half of the butter until golden, stirring often. Add the beef stock and boil 15 minutes. Season to taste with salt and pepper. Place the pieces of toast in 1 large or 4 small casseroles. Add the soup and sprinkle lavishly with cheese. Dot with the remaining bits of butter. Bake in an oven preheated 400° until the top is golden brown. *Serves 4.*

MENU:

ONION SOUP
CHICKEN BREAST BASTED WITH BUTTER AND VERMOUTH
SPINACH PANCAKES
BLACK-BOTTOM PIE

TURTLE SOUP

This is one of the finest and one of the most expensive preludes to a superb meal. It would be wasteful to cook this if the rest of the meal was not in the same class and was anticlimatic. In these days when kitchens are either elaborate status symbols which shouldn't be mussed up or the usual cramped kitchens in apartments, no one or almost no one would try to prepare turtles at home from scratch. One buys the meat, in rather expensive cans, with an absence of clutter and the tedious preparation already done.

1 pound green turtle or terrapin meat, cut into pieces
3 cups water
3 cups brown stock
1 bay leaf
1 sprig thyme
2 cloves
¼ teaspoon allspice
Juice and thinly sliced peel of ½ lemon
A few grains cayenne
¼ teaspoon freshly ground black pepper
½ teaspoon salt
4 whole coriander pods
2 tablespoons cooking oil
2 medium onions, chopped
1 tablespoon flour
1½ cups fresh skinned seeded tomatoes
1 tablespoon chopped parsley
2 cloves minced garlic
Dry sherry
2 chopped hard-cooked eggs
Lemon slices

Place the turtle or terrapin meat, water, brown stock, bay leaf, fresh thyme, cloves, allspice, lemon juice and peel, cayenne, ground pepper, salt and coriander pods in a saucepan and bring to the boiling point. The coriander pods will rise to the top by the end of the cooking period and can be skimmed out before serving. Next heat the cooking oil and sauté the onion in it. Stir in the flour and add the tomatoes. Permit these ingredients to cook over low heat for 10 minutes. Combine them with the turtle mixture, parsley and garlic. Simmer the soup until the meat is tender, at least 2 hours. You can add a few drops of caramel coloring. Add to each serving 1 or 2 tablespoons of dry sherry and garnish the soup with the eggs and lemon slices. *Serves 6 to 8.*

MENU:

TURTLE SOUP
FILET OF BEEF WELLINGTON
ENDIVE SALAD
GRAND-MARNIER SOUFFLÉ

CUCUMBER AND PORK SOUP

A delicate and different Chinese combination simple to prepare and lovely to look at.

2 cucumbers
2 medium pork chops
4 cups beef stock
1 teaspoon salt
¼ teaspoon monosodium glutamate

Peel the cucumbers in halves lengthwise. Remove the seeds and cut in thin slices, crosswise. Cut the bones and fat from the pork chops and slice the meat into strips about 1 inch × ¼ inch × ¼ inch. Heat the stock and salt. Bring to a boil. Add the pork strips and cook for 8 minutes. Add the cucumbers and bring to a boil again. Add the monosodium glutamate. The pork slices are thoroughly cooked after boiling in the soup for 8 minutes; the cucumbers about as soon as they are transparent, which is just a minute or two. *Serves 4.*

MENU:

CUCUMBER AND PORK SOUP
POLENTA WITH CHICKEN LIVERS
TOSSED SALAD
BROWN BETTY

WON TON SOUP

To a New York restaurateur, a dumpling is a dumpling is a dumpling when served in a soup—whether it be called won ton, kreplach, ravioli or by some other name. A menu in a Chinese restaurant will list won ton soup and put "kreplach" in parentheses, thinking the customer will know one or the other of the names.

Won ton wrappings

1 cup flour
½ teaspoon salt
1 egg

Filling

½ pound ground pork
1 tablespoon dry sherry
1 tablespoon soy sauce
½ teaspoon salt
½ teaspoon sugar
¼ teaspoon monosodium glutamate

Soup

3 cups chicken broth
16 won tons
1 tablespoon soy sauce
½ teaspoon salt
White pepper to taste
1 scallion, chopped

Make the wrappings for the won tons first. Sift the flour and salt into a mixing bowl. Add the egg and knead. Sprinkle a little flour on a breadboard and knead the dough again until smooth. Cover the dough with a wet towel and let stand for 40 minutes. Roll the dough out paper thin and cut into 4-inch squares. Mix the ingredients for the filling in a bowl. Put ½ teaspoon of filling on each square. Fold in half and press the edges together, dampening with water. Bring 3 quarts of water to a boil. Add the won tons and bring to a boil again. The won tons will float to the surface. Add ½ cup cold water and bring to a boil once more. This last boil makes sure that the filling will be thoroughly cooked. When the won tons float to the surface again, they are ready. Drain and reserve. Heat the chicken broth in another pan with the soy sauce and salt. Drop the cooked won tons into the broth for a few minutes with the chopped scallion and serve. Won tons can be made in large batches and frozen. Cook them in boiling water without thawing. The wrappings for won tons can be bought in Chinese food stores in large cities. *Serves 4.*

MENU:

WON TON SOUP
BROILED SWORDFISH STEAKS
POPPYSEED NOODLES
TANGERINE SEGMENTS, CHOPPED CELERY, BLACK OLIVES AND SLIVERED ALMONDS WITH FRENCH DRESSING

CONSOMMÉ MADRILENE

This can be bought in cans, and some brands are good, but it tastes much fresher and more exciting when made with fresh tomatoes and canned or homemade beef consommé.

*3 cups homemade beef stock**
or
2 cans beef consommé

2 small tomatoes
Finely chopped parsley
Finely chopped chives
1 tablespoon port wine

Heat the beef stock or consommé. Drop the tomatoes in boiling water in another pan for a minute or two. Remove and skin. Cut the tomatoes in half and squeeze the seeds and juice into the consommé, adding the skins. Dice the tomatoes and put aside for garnish. Simmer the consommé for about 10 minutes. Strain, add the tomatoes, parsley, chives and port. Serve hot or cold. *Serves 4.*

MENU:

CONSOMMÉ MADRILENE
ROAST PORK
BLACK-EYED PEAS AND RICE
WATERCRESS WITH GRAPEFRUIT SEGMENTS, SLICED AVOCADOS AND FRENCH DRESSING

PERSIAN ONION SOUP

An amazingly delectable soup that might be described as a blend of the Greek avgolemono, sautéed onions and the Persian soup spice of mint, cinnamon and pepper. It is refreshingly different from the better known French onion soup. Pideh, a flat bread common to Near Eastern countries, can be bought in stores carrying Near Eastern foods.

4 medium onions, sliced
5 tablespoons oil
3 tablespoons flour
1½ teaspoons salt
½ teaspoon pepper
½ teaspoon turmeric
⅓ cup sugar
½ cup lime and lemon juice
2 eggs

Soup Spice

1 tablespoon dried mint
¼ teaspoon cinnamon
¼ teaspoon pepper

Sauté the onion in oil in a large pot for about 5 to 10 minutes. Mix the flour with a cup of water and add it to the sautéed onion. Add 5 cups more of water, the salt, pepper and turmeric. Simmer over low heat for 35 to 40 minutes. Add the sugar and lime and lemon juice to the soup and simmer for 10 to 15 minutes more. Rub the dried mint in the palm of your hand to make it powdery. Add the cinnamon and pepper to the mint and add to the soup before removing it from the fire. Beat the eggs. Add a ladle of soup to the eggs, beat and add to the soup. *Serves 4 or 5.*

MENU:

PERSIAN ONION SOUP
PIDEH
VEGETABLE SALAD (romaine lettuce, sliced cucumbers, tomato quarters, chopped green onions, sliced radishes, chopped parsley, chopped fresh dill or dill weed, chopped fresh mint leaves or dry mint and white goat cheese)
COFFEE ICE CREAM WITH CRÈME DE CACAO AND SHAVED BITTER CHOCOLATE

CONSOMMÉ SHERBET

A fresh and frosty way to begin a summer meal.

1 small onion, finely chopped
1 can beef consommé
1 can chicken consommé
1 tablespoon sugar
½ teaspoon salt
Pinch of savory
Pinch of thyme
Pinch of marjoram
Pinch of rosemary
1 teaspoon gelatin
½ cup sour cream
2 egg whites, stiffly beaten
Slivered lemon peel

Simmer the onion, beef and chicken consommé, sugar, salt and seasonings for 30 minutes. Meanwhile soften the gelatin in 2 tablespoons of cold water. Strain the consommé mixture. Add the softened gelatin to the hot consommé and stir until dissolved. Let cool slightly, turn into a freezing tray. Turn the temperature up to the highest mark. When it starts to freeze around the edges, remove from tray, beat with a rotary beater. Add the sour cream and fold in the stiffly beaten egg whites and freeze until firm. This will not get absolutely hard but rather frosty-looking. Sprinkle each serving with slivered lemon peel. *Serves 4 to 6.*

MENU:

CONSOMMÉ SHERBET
HAM SOUFFLÉ
BROCCOLI WITH LEMON JUICE AND BUTTER
BLUEBERRY TARTS

WATERCRESS AND FISH BALL SOUP

Oriental soups are often so delicate in appearance and substance that it is astonishing to find them so unexpectedly flavorful. The canned fish balls from Norway or Denmark can be bought in food specialty stores and are used by the canny Chinese here.

1 small can fish balls
1 tablespoon dry sherry
3 cups clear chicken broth, canned or homemade
1 teaspoon salt
1 bunch watercress, broken into 2-inch pieces

Rinse and drain the fish balls and cut them in half. Sprinkle with the sherry. Heat the broth; then add the fish balls, salt and watercress. Heat briefly. *Serves 4.*

MENU:

WATERCRESS AND FISH BALL SOUP
SHRIMP PILAF
AVOCADO SALAD
LEMON MERINGUE PIE

AVGOLEMONO SOUP
(Greek Egg and Lemon Soup)

One of the truly great and yet simple soups of the world.

8 cups strong clear chicken broth, canned or homemade
½ cup rice
4 eggs
Juice of 2 lemons
Parsley clusters

Bring the broth to a boil, add the rice and cook until the rice is tender, about 20 to 30 minutes. Turn the heat down. Beat the eggs with a rotary beater until light and foamy. Add the lemon juice and beat some more. Add 2 cups of the hot soup and beat until well mixed. Or put the eggs and lemon juice in a blender, cover and blend 1 minute, remove the top and add the 2 cups of soup while the blender is going. Add the diluted egg-and-lemon mixture to the rest of the soup, beating constantly. Heat almost to the boiling point but not quite or the soup will curdle. Serve it immediately, sprinkled with parsley clusters. *Serves 6 to 8.*

MENU:

AVGOLEMONO SOUP
BROILED SALMON STEAKS WITH ANCHOVY BUTTER
CREAMED SPINACH
TINY BOILED NEW POTATOES
CHERRY TURNOVERS

JAPANESE SOUP

An elegant and simple and distinguished Japanese soup. It seems incredible that a soup with so few and such simple ingredients should have flavor, but it does indeed.

5 shrimp
1 small onion, sliced paper-thin
Sliced carrot with serrated edges
1 stalk celery
Salt
Pinch of sugar
Dash of soy sauce
1 egg, beaten
Thin pieces lemon peel
Juice of ½ lemon
4 sprigs parsley

Simmer the shrimp, onion, carrot, celery, salt, sugar and soy sauce in 4 cups or more of water. Simmer until the vegetables are barely tender. Remove the celery, add a spoonful of the broth to the well-beaten egg-yolk mix and add to the soup. When serving, put a few pieces of lemon peel with a dash of lemon juice and a sprig of parsley in each cup. This should be served in small thin bowls available in Oriental stores everywhere. *Serves 4.*

MENU:

JAPANESE SOUP LAMB STEW
SLICED ORANGE AND ONION SALAD WITH FRENCH DRESSING AND CHOPPED MINT
FRENCH BREAD CHOCOLATE MOUSSE

CLAM AND TOMATO BROTH WITH CURRIED CLAM CUSTARD

A celestial, unstereotyped, delicate and spicy beginning of a meal. Fancy vegetable cutters, which can be bought in well-stocked kitchen supply stores, can be used to cut the custard into fancy shapes, or it can be cut into diamonds or squares about a half inch long with a knife.

1 pint clam juice
1 pint tomato juice
½ bay leaf
½ teaspoon grated lemon peel

Heat the clam and tomato juices with the bay leaf and grated lemon peel. Check the seasonings—commercial tomato juices vary somewhat in flavor and seasoning—and add more if necessary. Remove the bay leaf and serve with tiny pieces of curried clam custard.

Curried Clam Custard

1 egg
2 egg yolks
¾ teaspoon salt
1½ teaspoons curry powder
1 can minced clams (drain and save the juice)
1 tablespoon sherry

Beat the eggs thoroughly. Add ½ cup of the clam juice. Add the salt, curry powder, clams and sherry. Beat well and pour into a greased shallow pan about ½ inch deep. Set in a larger pan of hot water. Cover and steam over low heat for 25 minutes or until a knife inserted in the custard comes out clean. This can be made ahead and chilled. To serve, cut into small diamonds or other shapes with vegetable cutters. Serve 3 or 4 pieces in each soup bowl. *Serves 4 to 6.*

MENU:

CLAM AND TOMATO BROTH WITH CURRIED CLAM CUSTARD
BROILED BABY TURKEY
BROCCOLI WITH LEMON BUTTER SAUCE
CORN PUDDING
FRESH PINEAPPLE CHUNKS
CHOCOLATE LEAVES

SOU CHAN'S HAM AND MUSTARD SOUP

The delicate and almost haunting flavor of Oriental soups such as this continues to astonish and delight Occidental devotees.

¼ pound Virginia ham, cut into 1½ × 2-inch pieces
1 quart chicken or beef stock
1 piece of ginger root or *½ teaspoon ground ginger*
Salt, if necessary
½ pound mustard greens cut into 1½-inch pieces

Simmer the ham in the stock with the ginger and salt for 15 minutes. Remove the ham, add the mustard greens, bring to a boil for 2 or 3 minutes. Stir but do not cover. Add the ham and serve. *Serves 4.*

MENU:

SOU CHAN'S HAM AND MUSTARD SOUP
SWEET AND PUNGENT PORK
DICED CHICKEN WITH ALMONDS
RICE
FORTUNE COOKIES

JELLIED CHICKEN CONSOMMÉ WITH RAW MUSHROOMS

For me, the flavor of raw mushrooms is exciting in a subtle way. There is a slightly nutty flavor and an elusive aroma, like the heady, earthy odor of a greenhouse or conservatory.

2 cans clear chicken consommé or broth, homemade or canned
¼ pound fresh mushrooms, sliced
3 tablespoons lemon juice
1 tablespoon finely chopped chives

Chill the chicken broth until firm but still quivery. Sprinkle the mushrooms with lemon juice to keep them from changing color. Spoon the jellied broth into small bowls with the mushrooms, between spoonfuls of the jelly. The mushrooms should be placed somewhat asymmetrically at different levels. This looks well in small glass bowls, sherbet glasses or even large wineglasses. Sprinkle the tops with finely chopped chives. *Serves 4.*

MENU:

JELLIED CHICKEN CONSOMMÉ WITH RAW MUSHROOMS

HOT BROWN 'N' SERVE FRENCH ROLLS

VEAL PICCATA

GREEN NOODLES WITH BUTTER AND CHEESE

MARINATED ARTICHOKE HEARTS

RASPBERRY SOUFFLÉ

2

Soups That Soothe Body and Spirits

All soups are somewhat soothing but there are some, such as vichyssoise, that seem to banish the frets of daily life while one sips. It is almost a physical thing that can be felt as they go down.

POTAGE BONNE FEMME

It is said that Madame de Pompadour created a soup of this name when she was winning the heart of Louis XV and influencing him. Other soups that also go by this name include leeks and potatoes.

- *1 white heart of lettuce, shredded*
- *1 small cucumber, peeled, quartered and sliced*
- *3 tablespoons unsalted butter*
- *2 sprigs fresh tarragon, chopped*
- *1 teaspoon finely chopped parsley*
- *5 cups chicken or veal broth*
- *2 egg yolks, slightly beaten*
- *½ cup heavy cream*
- *Salt and pepper*
- *Pinch of nutmeg*
- *More chopped parsley or chervil*

Sauté the shredded lettuce and ¼ of the cucumber in the sweet butter for 2 or 3 minutes. Add the tarragon and parsley and cook for a couple of minutes more. Add the chicken or veal broth and the rest of the cucumber. Cook over low heat for about 15 minutes or until the vegetables are tender. Mix the beaten egg yolks with the heavy cream and blend well. Remove the soup from the fire and stir in the egg-cream mixture, whipping with a wire whisk until smooth and thickened. Add the salt, pepper and nutmeg. Serve at once in warm soup plates sprinkled with the finely chopped parsley or chervil, if available. *Serves 4 to 6.*

MENU:

POTAGE BONNE FEMME

HOT BACON BISCUITS

POACHED SALMON STEAKS WITH AMANDINE SAUCE

CURRANT AND NUT PILAF

MELON

COLD CUCUMBER AND BUTTERMILK SOUP

This blissful and tranquilizing soup in no danger of interference from the Federal Food and Drug Administration.

2 small tender cucumbers, peeled and finely diced
⅔ cup seedless raisins, cut in half
1 quart buttermilk
Salt
Coarsely ground black pepper
Finely chopped fresh dill

Put the cucumbers in a bowl and chill well with some ice cubes on top of them. Drain the cucumbers thoroughly, add the raisins and buttermilk. Season with salt and pepper and serve in chilled cups with the chopped dill on top. *Serves 6.*

MENU:

COLD CUCUMBER AND BUTTERMILK SOUP
SHRIMP CREOLE
PORTUGUESE BREAD
SPANISH FLAN WITH CARAMEL SAUCE

OKROSHKA

Okroshka, one of the few substantial cold soups, is of Russian origin and is found in Poland and other bordering countries, too. Traditionally, it is made with kvass, a fermented drink made from black bread. Kvass can be found in New York City, but Americans are not fond of it and neither are some Russians. Often sour cream is diluted with white wine and some sparkling water. I prefer buttermilk undiluted.

⅓ cup chopped green onions, with tops and bottoms
1 teaspoon chopped fresh tarragon
3 tablespoons chopped fresh dill
or
½ teaspoon crushed dill weed
1 teaspoon salt
1 teaspoon sugar
Freshly ground black pepper
1 tablespoon prepared mustard
1 tablespoon lemon juice
1 tablespoon vinegar
2 cups diced cooked meat (roast beef, chicken or veal)
1 quart buttermilk
or
1 pint sour cream, thinned with 1 cup bouillon and 1 cup white wine
2 cups diced cucumbers
½ dill pickle, chopped
Ice cubes
2 hard-cooked eggs, sliced
2 tablespoons finely chopped parsley

Put the green onions, tarragon, fresh dill or crushed dill weed, salt, sugar, black pepper, mustard, lemon juice and vinegar in a bowl and stir with a wooden spoon. Add cooked meat, buttermilk or diluted sour cream, diced cucumber and dill pickle and chill. Serve in large shallow bowls which have also been chilled. Put an ice cube in each of the bowls. Pour in the soup mixture, making certain that each bowl has some of everything. Float a few slices of egg in the bowls. Sprinkle with parsley. *Serves 4.*

MENU:

OKROSHKA
COLD BAKED TOMATOES STUFFED WITH SPINACH
FRESH PEACH SHORTCAKE

CRÈME CYRANO

While this is served as a soup, in reality it is an unsweetened chicken custard. Served cold on a hot day, it is a most delectable beginning to a meal. In some versions it is baked in the manner of the dessert custards. In this, it is cooked like a so-called "boiled" custard, which, of course, is never permitted to boil.

4 large or 5 medium egg yolks
Salt
Pinch of cayenne pepper
2 cups hot chicken broth, canned or homemade
1 cup heavy cream
Tarragon leaves (fresh or preserved in vinegar)
Slivered almonds

Beat the egg yolks with the salt and cayenne pepper, and add the chicken broth or put into blender and blend. Cook in the top of a double boiler over hot water, stirring until thick. Do not let it boil. Add the cream and stir some more. Fill custard cups or Japanese handleless teacups with the mixture. Arrange the tarragon leaves and slivered almonds on top in a pleasing design. Chill thoroughly. *Serves 4 to 6.*

MENU:

CRÈME CYRANO
MARYLAND CRAB CAKES
COLE SLAW
FRENCH FRIES
HOT BACON BISCUITS
HONEYDEW MELON

COLD GREEN BEAN SOUP

On a hot summer day when the body is too sluggish to contend with the digestive demands of a complex meal, try a simple, soothing cold green bean soup, Hungarian style, with good crusty bread, some good cheese at room temperature and a bottle of cold white wine.

1 pound green beans, cut into pieces or Frenched
or
1 box frozen cut or Frenched beans
4 or 5 thin strips lemon peel
1 bay leaf
1 cup milk
1 cup sour cream
1 egg yolk
1 tablespoon lemon juice
Salt
Freshly ground black pepper

Cook the beans in 3 cups of water with the lemon peel and bay leaf until the beans are barely tender. This will vary with the age and size of the beans. Drain the beans and save the liquid. Remove and discard the lemon peel and bay leaf. Add the milk and sour cream to the bean liquid. Mix the egg yolk and lemon juice together and stir into the liquid when slightly cool. Season with salt and lots of pepper. Add the beans and chill for several hours. Serve cold in pretty bowls. *Serves 4.*

MENU:

COLD GREEN BEAN SOUP
SHARP CHEDDAR CHEESE
FRENCH BREAD
CHABLIS

CREAM OF ARTICHOKE SOUP

This can be made simply this way with frozen artichoke hearts and chicken broth or somewhat more tediously with the whole artichokes. The texture in each case is different, but the flavor is subtle whichever way it is made.

1 package frozen artichoke hearts, quartered
3 cups chicken broth
2 green onions, minced
2 tablespoons butter
1 tablespoon flour
1 cup coffee cream
Salt and white pepper (if necessary)
1 canned whole pimento, cut into stars or crescents (nice but not obligatory)

Simmer the frozen artichoke hearts in the chicken broth in a covered saucepan for ½ hour. Put through a fine sieve or purée in a blender. Sauté the onions in the butter, sprinkle with the flour and stir. Return artichokes to the heat, add the cream and sautéed onions. Season with salt and white pepper if necessary. Float the pimento stars on top. *Serves 4 to 6.*

MENU:

CREAM OF ARTICHOKE SOUP
BROILED SALMON STEAKS
BOILED NEW POTATOES
BIBB LETTUCE SALAD
STRAWBERRY SHORTCAKE MADE WITH DROP BISCUITS

SENEGALESE SOUP

This classic combination of flavors is truly great. It is best, as all dishes are, when made of the best ingredients—the very finest homemade chicken broth, the best curry powder and so on, but it is a difficult dish to spoil.

2 medium onions, chopped
3 stalks celery, chopped
4 tablespoons butter
1 tablespoon curry powder
6 cups chicken broth, canned or homemade
1 bay leaf
2 apples, peeled and chopped
1 cup light cream
1 cup cooked chicken, cut julienne or matchstick style

Sauté the onion and celery in the butter until limp. Add the curry powder and cook over low heat, stirring, for 5 minutes. Add the broth, bay leaf and apples. Simmer for 30 to 40 minutes or until the vegetables are mushy. Strain and chill. Before serving, add the cream and julienne chicken. *Serves 6 to 8.*

MENU:

SENEGALESE SOUP BROILED PORK CHOPS
BROILED APRICOT HALVES BAKED SWEET POTATOES
FRESH STRAWBERRIES

JULIA CHILD'S VICHYSSOISE WITH JULIENNE PICKLED BEETS

Julia Child, who conducts a TV cooking program with verve, dash, imagination and good-humored ease, suggested this garnish on one of her programs.

1 can frozen condensed cream of potato soup
1 soup can half milk, half sour cream

Pickled beets, cut julienne
or
Cucumber, cut julienne and sprinkled with salt and vinegar

Dilute the cream of potato soup with the milk and sour cream. Heat first, then chill. Serve the soup and sprinkle the beets or cucumber enough to be decorative on top. *Serves 4.*

MENU:

JULIA CHILD'S VICHYSSOISE WITH JULIENNE PICKLED BEETS
BROILED STEAKS
BROILED TOMATOES
SAUTÉED ROUNDS OF EGGPLANT
RASPBERRY TURNOVERS

BULGARIAN CUCUMBER SOUP

Cooking and eating these days are adventurous and free-swinging, and include dishes from all over the world rather than one section of our own country. A Bulgarian cucumber soup fits in quite well with a not too timid cuisine.

1 clove garlic, crushed
½ teaspoon salt
2 tablespoons oil
2 containers yoghurt
1 cucumber, peeled and minced
Lemon juice to taste
Freshly ground black pepper
½ cup chopped walnuts
Ice water
Chopped parsley
1 cup chopped ice

Stir the garlic with the salt, add the oil and yoghurt and stir until smooth. Add the cucumber, lemon juice, pepper, nuts and enough ice water to make 4 cups. Pour into cold cups and strew lightly with parsley. Add some chopped ice to each serving. *Serves 4 to 6.*

MENU:

BULGARIAN CUCUMBER SOUP
BARBECUED CHICKEN
RICE AND MUSHROOM PILAF
LETTUCE WITH LEMON CREAM DRESSING
CHEESECAKE

CREAM OF ASPARAGUS SOUP

Undoubtedly there is not a single grocery store in the United States, whether a supermarket or a tiny hole-in-the-wall delicatessen, that does not have at least one brand, or even several brands of canned cream of asparagus soup—and most brands are very good. But somehow the homemade soups made with fresh asparagus taste like an entirely different soup.

1 pound fresh green asparagus
Milk or water
6 cups veal or chicken stock
¼ cup chopped onion
½ cup chopped celery
3 tablespoons butter
3 tablespoons flour
½ cup cream
Salt, paprika and white pepper
1 hard-cooked egg, diced

Wash and remove the tips from the asparagus. Simmer the tips, covered, until they are tender, in a small amount of milk or water. Drain and save. Cut the stalks into pieces and place them in a saucepan with the veal or chicken stock, onion and celery. Simmer these ingredients, covered, for about ½ hour. Rub them through a sieve. Melt the butter and then stir in, until blended, the flour and cream. Add the asparagus stock. Heat the soup well in a double boiler. Add the asparagus tips. Season the soup immediately before serving with the salt, paprika and white pepper. Garnish with the diced egg. Serve in cups. *Serves 6.*

MENU:

CREAM OF FRESH ASPARAGUS SOUP
VEAL WITH RICE AND SOUR CREAM
COLD MARINATED GREEN BEANS WITH BLACK WALNUTS
APRICOT MOUSSE

TURNIP SOUP

Made with small white turnips, not the big woody winter ones, this is unbelievably good in a creamy, buttery way.

2 cups turnips, peeled and diced
1 quart beef broth
1 cup heavy cream
Salt
Freshly ground black pepper
2 egg yolks, beaten
1 tablespoon butter

Cook the turnips in the beef broth until tender. Drain, reserving the liquid. Rub the turnips through a sieve or food mill, or purée in a blender. Add the cooking liquid to the puréed turnips and bring to a boil. Remove from the heat, add the cream and season to taste with salt and pepper. Reheat but do not boil. Remove from the heat and stir in the egg yolks and butter. Serve piping hot. *Serves 6.*

MENU:

TURNIP SOUP
JAMBALAYA
LEMON SHERBET WITH WHITE GRAPES

POTAGE BAGRATION

We don't know why the French are inclined to name recipes after battles or generals, even a Russian one. Offhand, there don't seem to be any recipes named for Bull Run, Yorktown, John Paul Jones, Von Steuben, etc. This is neither a timesaving soup nor a laborsaving one, nor a frugal one—just a superb one.

½ pound veal cutlet, cubed
2 tablespoons butter
Sauce velouté
2 egg yolks
½ cup heavy cream
1 tablespoon butter
½ cup cooked macaroni
Grated Parmesan cheese

Brown the veal cubes in butter over high heat. Add the sauce velouté and cook slowly for 1½ hours or until the veal is very tender. Purée the soup in a blender or force it through a fine sieve. At this point the soup should be rather thin; add a little more stock if it isn't. Then thicken the soup, with the egg yolks beaten with the cream. Cook over low heat and add the butter in little pieces. Garnish with the macaroni cut into small pieces. Serve the grated Parmesan cheese separately. *Serves 6.*

Sauce Velouté

4 tablespoons butter
4 tablespoons flour
*4 cups veal stock**
4 tablespoons heavy cream
Salt and white pepper

Melt the butter in a heavy saucepan and stir in the flour. Cook stirring constantly for about 2 minutes without letting it color. Add the veal stock gradually, stirring with a whisk and then add the cream, and salt and pepper to taste. Cook until the sauce is thickened and smooth.

MENU:

POTAGE BAGRATION
ROAST SALMON HAUNCH
LIMA BEANS IN BUTTER SAUCE
CUCUMBER AND WATERCRESS SALAD   LEMON SOUFFLÉ

GAZPACHO

Gazpacho is so ubiquitous in this country and in Spain that it seems almost superfluous to give still another recipe. On the other hand, no self-respecting book on soups should be without one.

1 clove garlic
1 medium onion, coarsely chopped
3 tomatoes, peeled and quartered
1 cucumber, peeled and diced
½ large sweet red or green pepper, shredded
2 tablespoons good olive oil
2 tablespoons wine vinegar
½ cup ice water
1 teaspoon oregano
½ teaspoon salt cayenne
½ cup dry bread cubes
Ice cubes

Put everything in a blender except the ice cubes and bread cubes, and blend until smooth. You can also mince this very fine, pound it in a mortar or put it through a food mill. Chill well and serve with an ice cube in each bowl, and top with the bread cubes. *Serves 4.*

MENU:

GAZPACHO   SHRIMP CURRY
RICE   BAKED CUSTARD

PURÉE LÉONTINE

It is sad that leeks, which are so easily available in Europe, are often difficult to find here—except in our most cosmopolitan cities, where they are expensive. Green scallions are an acceptable substitute, but their flavor and texture are different, though good in their way.

¼ cup olive oil
2 pounds leeks or 2 or 3 bunches green onions, cleaned and cut into pieces
Salt and pepper
2 tablespoons lemon juice
1 cup shredded spinach
1 cup green peas
1 cup shredded lettuce
1 tablespoon chopped parsley
1 tablespoon chopped mint
1 tablespoon chopped celery

Put the olive oil into a soup pot, add the leeks or onions, salt, pepper and lemon juice. Simmer slowly for about 20 minutes. Then add the spinach, peas, lettuce and 4 cups of water. Cook until all the vegetables are soft, about 10 minutes, then put through a food mill or in a blender. If too thick, add a little milk or stock. Before serving, stir in the chopped parsley, mint and celery. *Serves 6.*

MENU:

PURÉE LÉONTINE
GRILLED FLOUNDER
EGGPLANT IN CHEESE SAUCE
BAKED APPLES FILLED WITH GINGER MARMALADE

POTAGE SAINT-GERMAIN

Sometimes the French get tired of saying that this delectable soup is *not* the same as that made with dried peas, good as that is. It is at its celestial best when made with fresh peas, as fresh as you can get them, but a pleasing version can be made with frozen peas. It is not the same, though.

½ cup (1 stick) butter
1 small head Boston lettuce, cut into pieces
1½ pounds fresh peas, shelled
or
1 (12-ounce) package frozen peas
2 teaspoons salt
1 tablespoon sugar
2 or 3 sprigs watercress
3 cups chicken broth or water

Melt the butter and cook the lettuce briefly in it with the peas. Put the lettuce and peas in a blender with the salt, sugar, watercress and 1 cup of the chicken broth or water and blend until smooth, or purée in a food mill. Put back in the pan with the rest of the chicken broth. Bring to a boil, turn the heat down and simmer gently for 10 to 15 minutes. *Serves 4.*

MENU:

POTAGE SAINT-GERMAIN SALT STICKS
ROAST CHICKEN ARTICHOKES WITH BUTTER
NOODLES MACAROON CUSTARD

ARMENIAN BARLEY AND YOGHURT SOUP

No matter how much one likes the more relaxed tempo and ways of summer, there come times when the heat is just too much, when ordinarily kind people start snapping at each other. One of the more blissful ways of achieving serenity is a cold bowl of barley and yoghurt soup. Most large cities have restaurants of some Near Eastern variation that serve this, or it can easily be made at home.

1 cup barley
6 cups beef or chicken stock
¼ cup (½ stick) butter
1 cup chopped onion
2 tablespoons chopped parsley
1 tablespoon dried mint
Salt and pepper
1 quart yoghurt (that which comes in a glass jar seems to taste better)

Cook the barley in the stock. Sauté the onions in the butter until pale and translucent but not brown. Add to the barley and stock with the parsley, mint, salt and pepper. When the barley is tender, add the yoghurt and cook for 5 minutes longer. Serve hot immediately or best of all chill and serve for instant bliss. *Serves 6 to 8.*

MENU:

ARMENIAN BARLEY AND YOGHURT SOUP
EGGPLANT PARMESAN
SLICED ORANGES SPRINKLED WITH RUM

SHRIMP CHOWDER

Shrimp makes a fine chowder, especially when combined with corn. Because it is easy to overcook shrimp, begin with raw shrimp, either fresh or frozen as most of it is marketed these days.

4 tablespoons butter
¼ cup finely chopped onion
¼ cup finely chopped celery
1 pound raw shrimp, peeled and deveined
3 tablespoons flour
1 quart milk
1 cup niblet corn, canned or frozen
½ green bell pepper, cut into ½-inch strips
½ red bell pepper or 1 canned pimento, cut into ½-inch strips
Salt
Tabasco sauce
Paprika
2 cups heavy cream, lightly whipped

Cook the onion, celery and shrimp in the butter until the vegetables are pale yellow and the shrimp pale pink. Add the flour and stir to blend. Pour in the milk, corn and green and red pepper strips. Cook over low heat. Add salt and a cautious dash of Tabasco sauce. Sprinkle with paprika. Stir in the lightly whipped cream. *Serves 4 to 6.*

MENU:

SHRIMP CHOWDER   CORN MUFFINS
CUCUMBER AND WATERCRESS SALAD WITH FRENCH DRESSING
GRAPEFRUIT ALASKA

CREAM OF BROCCOLI SOUP

Someone said recently when the subject of this book was mentioned that soup was so *dull.* I think it one of the most exciting, one of the most varied, one of the most individual of dishes and one that gives the most pleasure in the making.

1 pound broccoli
4 tablespoons (½ stick) butter
6 tablespoons flour
6 cups chicken broth
1 cup heavy cream
2 egg yolks
Salt and pepper
Thin slices of lemon
Whipped cream

Cook the broccoli in 4 cups of boiling salted water until barely tender. Drain and save the cooking water. Melt the butter, blend in the flour and cook stirring constantly until well blended and golden but not brown. Add the chicken broth and 2 cups of the broccoli cooking water, stirring until smooth. Add the cooked broccoli except for a few of the flowerets which are saved for the garnish. Simmer the soup for 30 minutes. Put in the blender a little at a time or press through a fine sieve. Stir in the heavy cream that has been beaten with the egg yolks. Put the soup on the heat for a few minutes but do not let it come to a boil. Add salt and pepper to taste. Chill thoroughly. Garnish each soup bowl with a slice of lemon piled with salted whipped cream and one of the broccoli flowerets. *Serves 6 to 8.*

MENU:

CREAM OF BROCCOLI SOUP
VEAL SCALOPPINI
GREEN BEANS WITH WATER CHESTNUTS
PEARS WITH CHOCOLATE SAUCE

DANISH BROWN SOUP

(Brun Suppe med Parmesaabollar)

Brown soup has a very delicate flavor and is well known in Europe. It sounds rather odd to Americans, who usually enjoy it when they taste it. This Danish version is served in a lavish fashion with eggs stuffed with Parmesan cheese.

3 tablespoons butter
3 tablespoons flour
6 cups beef stock or bouillon
Salt
Pinch of cayenne pepper
2 tablespoons sherry

Melt the butter in a soup kettle, stir in the flour and let the mixture brown but not burn. Add the stock a little at a time, beating with a whisk. Boil for 10 to 15 minutes. It should be about the thickness of evaporated milk. Add more salt if the bouillon did not have enough and add a pinch of cayenne. Remove from the heat, add the sherry. Pour into warm soup plates. Add the stuffed eggs for a lavish version. *Serves 6.*

Stuffed Eggs

3 hard-cooked eggs
1 tablespoon melted butter
1½ tablespoons grated Parmesan cheese
Salt and pepper

Cut the eggs in half lengthwise. Remove the yolks to a small bowl, mash well with a fork and add the butter, then the cheese and the seasoning. Mix well and either pile into the egg whites or, more elegantly, do as the Danes do and make into 18 small balls. Place 3 balls on each egg white and put 1 egg white in each soup plate before pouring in the soup. *Serves 6.*

MENU:

DANISH BROWN SOUP
RYE BREAD ROLLS
ZWIEBELKÜCKEN OR SWISS ONION TART
FRESH FRUIT

CREAM OF FRESH TOMATO SOUP

In this packaged age, one can get anything from Swedish instant rose hip soup to instant snail butter from France, but homemade cream of tomato soup made from fresh tomatoes tastes like an entirely different soup from that which comes in cans.

4 large or 8 small tomatoes
¼ cup (½ stick) butter
¼ cup hot water
2 cups milk
2 cups half-and-half
1½ teaspoons dried tarragon
or
1 tablespoon chopped fresh tarragon
1 clove garlic
Salt and pepper

Quarter the tomatoes and squeeze out the seeds and juice and discard. Simmer the tomatoes in the butter in a covered pan until tender and thickened, about 20 minutes. Put through a sieve or purée in a blender and add the rest of the ingredients. The garlic clove can be cut in half and fished out later or squeezed in a garlic press. It is not quite as good that way but saves fishing for it later. *Serves 4.*

MENU:

CREAM OF FRESH TOMATO SOUP
LAMB CHOPS WITH WATERCRESS
BARLEY AND MUSHROOM CASSEROLE
BROILED GRAPEFRUIT WITH SHERRY

CREAM OF CAULIFLOWER SOUP

A creamy and dreamy soup.

1 medium head of cauliflower, about 2 pounds
2 tablespoons butter or bacon fat
2 tablespoons flour
4 cups milk
Salt and pepper
Slivered raw carrot

Separate the cauliflower flowerets, put in a pan with some water and cook until very soft. Drain and purée in a food mill or in a blender. Melt the butter or bacon fat, add the flour. Stir and cook for a few minutes, then add the milk slowly a little at a time. Add the puréed cauliflower, salt and pepper. Heat thoroughly while stirring well. Serve with scraped, slivered raw carrot sprinkled on top. *Serves 4.*

MENU:

CREAM OF CAULIFLOWER SOUP
SAUTÉED CANADIAN BACON
POTATO PANCAKES
APPLESAUCE
CHERRY STRUDEL

POTATO AND LETTUCE SOUP

Classic, soporific and simple, if the ancient belief in the soothing powers of lettuce is true. The pear and ginger sherbet can be made in the refrigerator very simply. Purée canned pears, add the juice and some diced crystallized ginger and freeze.

2 cups peeled and diced potatoes
1 medium onion, chopped fine
¼ bunch parsley, chopped fine
Bunch of chives, as thick as your thumb, minced
3 tablespoons butter
3 cups chicken stock
2 egg yolks, well beaten
1 cup milk
Heart of lettuce, torn apart into small pieces

Simmer the potatoes, onion, parsley, chives, butter and chicken stock until the potatoes are soft. Rub through a sieve or purée in a blender. Put the egg yolks mixed with the milk in a pan. Cook over low heat, stirring until smooth and thickened. Add potato-onion mixture, sprinkle the top with the lettuce and simmer for only 3 or 4 minutes more. *Serves 4 to 6.*

MENU:

POTATO AND LETTUCE SOUP
BROILED HAMBURGERS
SUCCOTASH WITH CHEESE SAUCE
PEAR AND GINGER SHERBET

CREAM OF SPINACH SOUP
(Swedish version)

A cream soup becomes a suave and elegant overture to a meal when served in the best large shallow soup plates with a stuffed egg in the center.

1 pound fresh spinach
3 tablespoons butter
½ teaspoon salt
2 tablespoons flour
1 cup milk
1½ cups beef consommé
1 cup light cream
1 teaspoon lemon juice
1 teaspoon sugar
*Stuffed eggs**

Cook the spinach in the butter with the salt until slightly wilted. Sprinkle with the flour and add the milk and consommé. Simmer for 15 to 20 minutes and purée in a blender or put through a food mill. Heat with the cream, lemon juice, sugar and more salt if needed. Serve with stuffed egg halves, one to each plate. *Serves 4.*

MENU:

CREAM OF SPINACH SOUP
FILLET OF FLOUNDER WITH WHITE GRAPES
BROILED TOMATOES PARSLEYED NEW POTATOES
PINEAPPLE SHERBET WITH GRATED ORANGE PEEL

COLD CHICKEN SOUP WITH CURRY

As all who live in hot countries know, highly seasoned dishes will rev up a system sluggish from heat.

1 large onion, chopped
3 tablespoons butter
1 tablespoon curry powder
1 can condensed cream of chicken soup
1 soup can chicken broth
½ cup white wine
1 cup cooked rice
1 cooked chicken breast, cut julienne
3 tablespoons toasted coconut
3 tablespoons crystallized ginger
⅓ cup canned sour red cherries, drained

Sauté the onion in the butter until lightly browned. Add the curry powder and stir well. Add the chicken soup and broth. Heat briefly with the white wine and the rice. Chill. When serving, put some of the julienne white meat in each bowl. Sprinkle with the toasted coconut, crystallized ginger and sour cherries. *Serves 4 on a day when it is really too hot to eat.*

MENU:

COLD CHICKEN SOUP WITH CURRY
THIN PARSLEY BUTTER SANDWICHES
WATERCRESS, GRAPEFRUIT SEGMENTS, GREEN ONION WITH FRENCH DRESSING
CRÈME BRULÉE

COLD BORSCHT WITH SOUR CREAM

One of the best of the uncomplicated soups, distinguished in its simplicity. It can be made with canned diced beets, still more simply.

5 medium beets, peeled and diced
Juice of 1 lemon
1 cucumber, peeled and cubed
2 spring onions, with tops and bottoms, chopped
Sour cream

Cook the beets in 1 quart of water with the lemon juice for 30 to 40 minutes or more until the beets are tender. Serve the liquid in chilled bowls with some of the chopped beets, cucumber, chopped spring onions and a good dollop of sour cream in each bowl. This soup can be kept in the refrigerator for several days. *Serves 4 to 6.*

MENU:

COLD BORSCHT WITH SOUR CREAM
ROAST CHICKEN
CORN BREAD STUFFING, BAKED SEPARATELY
CHICORY, AVOCADO AND WHITE GRAPE SALAD WITH FRENCH DRESSING
FRESH RASPBERRIES AND CREAM
POUND CAKE

COLD CUCUMBER SOUP

An amateur scientist who prefers to check his clichés for accuracy stuck thermometers in several cucumbers lying on the vine in the garden. He found they are indeed cooler than the surrounding temperature. Best of all, they make one feel cool and think cool.

2 cloves garlic, mashed in a mortar
2 tablespoons olive oil
1 large cucumber, peeled and diced
1 pint sour cream
1 teaspoon grated lemon peel

Beat everything in a bowl with about 6 ice cubes until the right consistency; it should be thick. Then throw away the ice cubes and serve completely cold. This doesn't work easily in a blender. *Serves 4.*

MENU:

COLD CUCUMBER SOUP
FRENCH BREAD
ROAST BEEF
NOODLES
COLD ARTICHOKES WITH MUSTARD MAYONNAISE
COLD MELON WITH PORT

COLD AVOCADO SOUP

A voluptuously bland soup with an artful, colorful and exciting topping of red caviar.

1 large or 2 medium ripe avocados
1 cup chicken broth, canned or homemade
1 cup heavy cream
2 teaspoons lemon juice
Salt and pepper
Red caviar
or
Finely chopped fresh dill or chives

Peel the avocado and put in a blender or through a food mill. Heat the puréed avocados with the chicken broth, stir until smooth and blended. Add the cream, lemon juice, salt and pepper. Stir and chill thoroughly. Serve sprinkled lavishly with the red caviar or more frugally but still delectably with the dill or chives. *Serves 4.*

MENU:

COLD AVOCADO SOUP WITH RED CAVIAR
BROILED STEAKS
BARLEY AND MUSHROOM CASSEROLE
WATERCRESS AND BIBB LETTUCE SALAD
CREAM PUFF SHELLS WITH STRAWBERRIES

VICHYSSOISE ACCORDING TO THE MASTER

Vichyssoise, first cousin to the French potage Parmentier, was devised by Louis Diat, chef of the old Ritz-Carlton in New York City, as a cold and soothing soup to have on a very hot day. The French, although not given to serving cold soups, are beginning to adopt it as their own.

4 leeks, white part only, sliced
1 medium onion, sliced
2 ounces (4 tablespoons) sweet butter
5 medium potatoes, peeled and sliced thin
1 quart water or chicken broth
1 tablespoon salt
3 cups milk
2 cups heavy cream
Finely chopped chives

Brown the leeks and onion in the sweet butter; then add the potatoes, water or chicken broth and salt. Boil from 35 to 40 minutes. Crush and rub through a fine strainer or purée in a blender. Chill well, add the milk and the heavy cream. Season to taste. Sprinkle with chopped chives. *Serves 6 to 8.*

MENU:

VICHYSSOISE ACCORDING TO THE MASTER
BROILED LAMB CHOPS
FRIED GREEN TOMATOES
CUCUMBER SALAD LIME PIE

3

Panaceas

These are the soups that are fine when one needs a restorative but doesn't want a meal or when one has been surfeited with too much rich food as when traveling or visiting or when one just wants something light and delicate. Toscanini always wanted the light and delicate soup included here before he conducted.

STRACCIATELLE

This is a fine dish to order in a restaurant in Italy or to prepare at home when exhausted, in low spirits, surfeited by too much rich food or weighted down by your own cares or those of the world. If your needs warrant, eat and serve with more grated Parmesan cheese, ripe olives, Italian bread and a glass of red wine. Otherwise serve it alone.

2 eggs
3 tablespoons freshly grated Parmesan cheese
¼ cup soft bread crumbs or farina
4 cups chicken broth, homemade or canned
Parsley

Beat the eggs in a bowl (not a blender) and add the grated Parmesan cheese and bread crumbs or farina. Add a cupful of the broth and stir until somewhat smooth. Heat the rest of the broth and when almost boiling, pour in the mixture and beat vigorously with a fork for 3 to 4 minutes. Then let the soup come just barely to a boil. The egg mixture should not be smooth but rather flaky. Sprinkle with parsley for a pleasing but unauthentic touch. Serve immediately. *Serves 4.*

CORN BREAD MILK TOAST

It is a moot question whether one is stretching a point by calling this a soup. It is hot and soothing and "knits up the ravell'd sleave of care," although sleep is not guaranteed. Since one day when there happened to be some leftover corn bread, I have used that instead of regular toast when possible. There are packaged corn bread disks or squares called "corn toasts" but you must toast them yourself. They are nice to have on hand when the world is too much with you.

2 squares corn bread or small muffins
or
2 corn toasts, toasted
1½ cups milk
1 tablespoon or more butter

Place the corn bread or corn toast in a soup bowl that has been warmed. Heat the milk with the butter until the milk is hot but not boiling. Pour over the corn bread and serve immediately with a glass of cold milk as an accompaniment. *Serves 1.*

TOSCANINI'S RICE AND CELERY SOUP

It is not likely that the soup served to Toscanini to warm and soothe him before he conducted a concert will change a normal consumer into a gifted conductor. The maestro did not go on to more food before a concert, but the less tense and less dedicated usually want more on a normal evening.

1 tablespoon butter
2 tablespoons celery, finely chopped
2 tablespoons rice
2 cups beef stock or canned bouillon
1 tablespoon finely chopped parsley

Melt the butter in a saucepan, add the celery and cook over low heat until tender. Add the rice and beef stock or bouillon; cover and simmer until rice is tender, about 20 minutes. Pour into bowl and sprinkle with parsley. Serve with hot toast. This is for one person in need of comfort. *Serves 1.*

MENU:

TOSCANINI'S RICE AND CELERY SOUP
POT ROAST WITH DUMPLINGS
BEET SALAD WITH SOUR CREAM DRESSING
PEAR AND CUSTARD TART

JAPANESE EGG GLOP SOUP

An authentic recipe if not an authentic title. Friends back from three years in Japan will have no other. It is a soothing and restorative soup, a panacea. It is an Oriental version of the Italian pavese, with soy sauce instead of grated cheese. Either soup is fine with or without some bread, with or without a glass of wine, and nothing else.

1 large onion, sliced
3 tablespoons butter
2 cans canned bouillon, diluted
or
5 cups homemade bouillon
¼ cup soy sauce
Salt and pepper, if necessary
4 eggs

Sauté the onion in the butter in a deep skillet until glazed. Add the bouillon diluted with water plus the soy sauce or the homemade bouillon and soy sauce. Season if necessary. Simmer for about 5 minutes. Lower the heat still more so that there is only the barest movement of the broth. Add the raw eggs to the broth, cover and poach for 3 to 5 minutes. Serve, allowing 1 egg to each serving. *Serves 4.*

MENU:

JAPANESE EGG GLOP SOUP
BREAD
WINE

PAVESE

In Italy when in need of being simply and instantly revitalized, one orders this fine simple dish. There is no reason why one must go to Italy in search of comfort when the ingredients are at hand in most homes.

1 egg
1¼ cups beef consommé
2 thick slices Italian bread, oven-toasted
Freshly grated Parmesan cheese

Poach the egg, separately. Sometimes it is done in the consommé, but it is not apt to get cooked that way. Heat the consommé separately. Place the poached egg in a warm soup bowl with a piece of toast on two sides. Sprinkle generously with the Parmesan cheese. Pour in the hot consommé. *Serves 1.*

BEEF TEA

In some period novels of the era around the turn of the century or even earlier, convalescents were often tempted to eat by being fed beef tea. It's a little expensive these days, but will make one seem born again when fed too long on invalid pap. Most versions start out with ground beef, but the one that has the most flavor is made with an inch-thick round steak that has been broiled first. Broil it for 2 minutes on each side. Cut it into inch squares. Put it into a pint jar and cover with cold water. Set that into a pan with cold water and let it steep, not boil, over low heat for 2 hours. Drain and salt the liquid when serving. *Makes 1 to 2 cups.*

GARLIC SOUP
(Aigo Buido)

Hot garlic soup is very reviving and is thought to be a fine cure for all sorts of ills. Although the amount of garlic sounds alarming, the flavor is so muted by the preliminary boiling that you might not suspect what it is that tastes so exquisite and delicately aromatic. Sometimes eggs beaten with olive oil are put into the tureen and rounds of toasted French bread with grated cheese accompany the soup. In Provençal, as in Spain, often poached eggs are served and cooked in the soup, much as for the Italian pavese. In this version, diced potatoes and saffron are cooked in the soup for the last 20 minutes and then served with French bread and grated cheese.

1 head garlic, separated but not peeled
2 teaspoons salt
Pinch of pepper
2 cloves
¼ teaspoon sage
¼ teaspoon thyme
½ bay leaf
4 sprigs parsley
3 tablespoons olive oil
3 cups peeled, diced potatoes
Pinch of saffron
Rounds of hard-toasted French bread
1 cup grated Swiss or Parmesan cheese

Put the garlic cloves in boiling water and boil for about a minute. Drain, run cold water over them to cool and peel. Put the peeled garlic in a saucepan with the seasonings, olive oil and 2 quarts of water. Boil slowly for 30 to 35 minutes. Add more seasoning if desired. Strain and return to the saucepan with the potatoes and saffron. Simmer for about 20 minutes or until the potatoes are tender. Check the seasoning again and serve with 3 slices of French bread in the bottom of each bowl sprinkled with some of the cheese. *Serves 6 to 8.*

MENU:

GARLIC SOUP
TOASTED FRENCH BREAD
GRATED SWISS OR PARMESAN CHEESE
PISSALADIÈRE
CHERRY TOMATOES
APRICOT COMPOTE

4

A Fine Kettle of Fish

Fish soups are so many and so varied in their ingredients and ways of cooking that they can and do fit into almost all classifications except, of course, the fruit soups. They are superb whether they are made on the beach from seafood just pulled from the sea or assembled from fresh, frozen or canned fish.

SOUPE DE POISSONS

This soup, in the manner of Provence, is made with fascinating little spiny fish of many varieties that are found around the Mediterranean. The broth is always strained, the fish discarded, and then pasta is cooked in it. This, so far from the Mediterranean and the fish there, is necessarily an adaption. Unlike those in bouillabaisse, the fish are never eaten, since they have given their all to the flavor of the broth.

1½ cups chopped onions
½ cup olive oil
4 cloves garlic, minced
1 pound ripe tomatoes, chopped and seeded
or
1 cup tomato purée
6 sprigs parsley
1 bay leaf
½ teaspoon thyme or basil
2 big pinches saffron
1 2-inch piece orange peel or 1 teaspoon grated orange peel
⅛ teaspoon pepper
1 tablespoon salt (omit if clam juice is used instead of fish broth)
3 to 4 pounds lean fish, fish heads, bones, etc.
or
1½ pounds frozen fish fillets (halibut, haddock, cod or perch)
or
1 quart clam juice plus 1½ quarts water and no salt
1 medium potato, peeled (remove and use for rouille)
1 cup small pasta shells
or
⅔ cup broken spaghetti or vermicelli
Toasted thick slices French bread
1 to 2 cups grated Swiss or Parmesan cheese
Rouille

Cook the onions in the olive oil until opaque but not brown. Add the garlic, tomatoes, herbs and seasonings. Cook over medium heat for 5 minutes. Add 2½ quarts water, the fish and bones, if any, or the clam juice and water. Cook uncovered at a slow boil for 30 to 40 minutes. Cook the potato in this liquid at the same time and remove when tender for the rouille. Strain the soup into another pan; check seasoning, adding more saffron if necessary. Add the pasta and boil for 10 to 20 minutes or until tender. The time will vary according to the size of the pasta. Check seasoning. Shellfish (mussels, shrimp, clam or lobster) can be used instead of part of the fish and put aside when the broth is strained, and added with the pasta. It is more usual to have the strained broth and pasta served over toasted thick French bread, sprinkled with grated Swiss or Parmesan cheese and with a spoon or two of rouille stirred in. The grated cheese and rouille are passed separately.

Rouille

¼ cup chopped sweet red pepper
or
¼ cup canned pimentos
1 small chili pepper, boiled until tender
or
A few drops of Tabasco sauce
1 medium potato, cooked in a soup (see above)
4 cloves minced garlic
1 teaspoon basil, thyme or savory
4 to 6 tablespoons olive oil
Salt and pepper
2 to 3 tablespoons hot soup

Simmer the pepper for several minutes in salted water and drain, or use drained and chopped canned pimentos. Put in a bowl with the cooked chili pepper, cooked potato, garlic and basil, thyme or savory. Pound together for several minutes to form a very smooth sticky sauce. Add the olive oil drop by drop, beating it in as if for mayonnaise. Just before serving, beat in the hot soup a little at a time and pour into a sauceboat or pitcher. This can of course be made in seconds, untraditionally, in a blender. Either way, it is served with fish, soup or bouillabaisse. Each person stirs it into his soup to taste. It should be very hot. Keep refrigerated when not in use. Will keep several weeks. *Serves 6 to 8.*

MENU:

SOUPE DE POISSONS
FRENCH BREAD
QUICHE LORRAINE
PEARS WITH CHOCOLATE SAUCE

MOULES MARINIÈRE

There is a mad mad race these days between the growing number of Americans who are learning to like mussels and gather them themselves along the shore and the dreadful pollution overtaking some of our coastal waters which makes the mussels unfit to eat. The safe way to gather unpolluted mussels is to check with the local health department. There are still places these days on the shores of the Long Island Sound where the mussels at low tide are as thick as poppy seeds. They are one of the most beautiful of our shellfish and thoroughly rewarding to clean and cook. The cleaning is a bit tedious and part of it is done for esthetic reasons. You scrape as many of the barnacles off as you have the will, using a dull knife, a wire suede brush or anything else.

3 quarts mussels
2 tablespoons butter
1 shallot, chopped
or
2 green onions, with tops and bottoms, chopped
1½ cups white wine
1 tablespoon finely chopped parsley

Scrape the mussels with a knife (see above), pulling out the beard or seaweedlike piece of each, and wash in several waters to get rid of all the grit. Discard any that float or are partly open. Melt the butter in a large wide pan. Add the shallot or onion. Cook for a minute or two but do not brown. Add the wine and clean drained mussels tight in their shells. Cook rather fast until the shells open. Then transfer them to a warm tureen or warm soup bowls. When all are opened, strain the mingled mussel juice and wine through cheesecloth to eliminate any sand and heat again. Pour over the mussels, which have been kept warm. Add the chopped parsley. Serve immediately in deep soup plates with plenty of French bread for mopping up the juices, oyster forks to remove the mussels from their shells, soupspoons for the juice and a bowl for the empty shells. Happy and uninhibited people sometimes use a shell as a soupspoon but not, of course, when dining formally. *Serves 4.*

MENU:

MOULES MARINIÈRE
BROILED LAMB CHOPS
BROILED TOMATO HALVES
CHEESE AND POTATO SOUFFLÉ
HONEYDEW MELON

PARTAN BREE OR CREAM OF CRAB SOUP

The Scots and the English have some fine and flourishing names for dishes that entrance those from other, supposedly linguistically allied countries. Among them are Partan Bree; bubble and squeak (a beef and cabbage dish); cullen skink (a perfectly normal fish chowder) and a dessert called whim-wham. The last was mentioned by Scott in *The Bride of Lammermore* and is not unlike the Italian dessert with the equally nonsensical title of zuppa inglese.

⅓ cup uncooked rice
2 cups milk
1 cup cream
1 pound crab meat, fresh or frozen or canned
1 tablespoon anchovy paste
Salt and white pepper

Cook the rice in the milk until soft. Push through a sieve or purée in a blender. Heat with the rest of the ingredients. Serve in small bowls. This is a very rich dish and very filling. *Serves 6 to 8.*

MENU:

PARTAN BREE
FRIED CHICKEN
SPINACH SOUFFLÉ
CHERRY TOMATOES
HONEYDEW MELON

BROWN OYSTER STEW WITH SESAME SEEDS

There is something very exciting about the sound of sesame when applied to seasoning, possibly because it reminds us subconsciously of all the color and mystery of *The Arabian Nights*. The seeds should be toasted first to bring out the flavoring. They enhance sauces, soups, salads, breads, cookies, candies and what not. In Charleston it's called benne seed and is sold there in many guises. The benne brittle is somewhat like peanut brittle but has a more subtle flavor and an interesting texture.

4 slices bacon, diced
1 large onion, chopped
2 tablespoons flour
2 cups oysters and their liquid
or
2 cans frozen oysters
2 tablespoons sesame seeds, toasted
White wine
Cooked rice or large cooked hominy
Chopped chives

Sauté the bacon and onion until brown. Remove from the pan with a slotted spoon. Sprinkle the flour into the grease and stir constantly until the flour is well browned. Remove from the stove. Mix the oyster liquid with enough wine to make 1½ cups in all. Add to the browned flour, little by little. Return to the fire and stir until slightly thickened. Add 1½ cups of water, a little at a time, stirring until smooth and thickened. Mash the sesame seeds in a mortar with a pestle or in a blender or with a blunt instrument.

Add to the soup. Add the onion, bacon and oysters. Cook until the edges of the oysters curl. Serve with a spoon of rice or hominy in each bowl and a sprinkling of chives. *Serves 4.*

MENU:

BROWN OYSTER STEW WITH SESAME SEEDS
HOT ROLLS
HAM-STUFFED VEAL
DEEP-FRIED EGGPLANT
FRESH FRUIT

MATELOTE

A classic French fish stew that is made traditionally with fresh-water fish and often eel cooked in red or white wine. The red is used most often. The fish is cut in thick slices.

1 large onion, finely chopped
2 cloves garlic, minced
3 tablespoons butter
2 tablespoons chopped parsley
1 bay leaf
1 sprig fresh dill
2 tablespoons chopped celery leaves
2 cups red or white wine
1 jigger brandy
Dusting of spices (pinch of nutmeg, ginger, cinnamon, pepper, very little salt)
10 to 12 small onions, boiled, then browned in butter
½ pound small mushrooms, cooked in the same butter
2 pounds fish, cut in thick slices, skin and all (usually some fresh-water fish such as carp, perch, or eel, but around the seacoast salt-water fish is used)

Sauté the onion and garlic in the butter, add the herbs, celery leaves, spices and wine. Bring to a boil. Light the brandy and pour it into the sauce. Simmer for about 30 minutes. Strain and put in another pan with the pieces of fish, small onions and mushrooms. Simmer for about 10 minutes. Serve with croutons. Some people prefer to thicken the stew with 4 tablespoons of butter mixed with 2 tablespoons of flour, but with the preliminary cooking of the sauce it is not necessary. *Serves 4 to 6.*

MENU:

MATELOTE
FRENCH BREAD
CORNMEAL PANCAKES FILLED WITH CREAMED CHICKEN
BAKED TOMATOES STUFFED WITH BACON AND CHOPPED SPINACH
HOT BROILED PEACH HALVES WITH CHOPPED PISTACHIO

BALKAN CHLODNIK

As with many Eastern European soups, one of the main ingredients of chlodnik is beets. If you have time and/or a garden, you begin with a bunch of beets and a pound of beet tops. If you are lazy, you begin with a large can of beets and a package of frozen spinach.

1 large can beets
1 pound young beet greens
or
1 package frozen chopped spinach
½ pound cooked shrimp, peeled and chopped
3 hard-cooked eggs, diced
1 cucumber, peeled, seeded and chopped
1 lemon, sliced thin
¼ cup finely chopped fresh dill
3 tablespoons chopped chives
4 cups sour cream
2 cups beer
Salt and pepper
Whole cooked shrimp

Chop the beets, put in a pan with the juice and chopped greens. Chopped spinach makes life a little simpler. Cook the greens with the beets and beet juice until barely tender, 5 to 10 minutes.

Remove from the heat and let cool. Add the chopped shrimp, diced eggs, chopped cucumber, lemon slices, dill and chives. Stir in the sour cream and beer. Season with salt and pepper. Stir well to blend. Chill the soup and serve with an ice cube in each bowl. Garnish with a few whole shrimp. *Serves 6 to 8.*

MENU:

BALKAN CHLODNIK
PUMPERNICKEL AND SWEET BREAD
ORANGE SLICES WITH RASPBERRIES

COLD NORWEGIAN FISH SOUP

It sometimes is difficult for some Protestants to understand why Catholics have thought it a discipline to eat fish. Many of the best soups in the world have fish as the main ingredient.

3 pounds fish with bones (cod, haddock, etc.)
2 onions, quartered
1 clove garlic
1 pint sour cream
Salt and pepper
1 teaspoon chopped chives
1 teaspoon dried tarragon leaves

Cook the fish with the bones, onions and garlic in enough cold water to cover amply until the flesh falls from the bones. Strain and chill. Mix the broth with the sour cream, salt and pepper. Serve sprinkled with chives and tarragon. *Serves 4 to 6.*

MENU:

COLD NORWEGIAN FISH SOUP
HOT FRENCH ROLLS
BOILED BEEF SALAD
FRESH ORANGES WITH MARMALADE

CHILLED SHRIMP BISQUE

A good meal for a hot but festive summer evening.

2 tablespoons quick-cooking tapioca
1¼ teaspoons salt
⅛ teaspoon pepper
⅛ teaspoon paprika
1 tablespoon minced onion
3 cups milk
1 cup light cream
1 cup cooked shrimp, washed, drained and cut into small pieces
⅓ cup finely chopped, sautéed fresh mushrooms
2 tablespoons butter
Light cream
Thin slices lemon or lime
Finely chopped parsley

Combine the tapioca, salt, pepper, paprika, onion, milk and cream in the top of a double boiler. Let the mixture stand for 15 minutes. Place it over rapidly boiling water and cook for 10 to 15 minutes, stirring frequently. Add the shrimp, mushrooms and butter and mix. Let stand over hot water for 15 to 20 minutes, to heat thoroughly and blend flavors. Cool. Then chill for 2 to 3 hours or overnight. Before serving, thin with cream to desired consistency. Serve in chilled cups or bowls. Top each serving with a slice of lemon or lime sprinkled with finely chopped parsley. *Serves 4 to 6.*

MENU:

CHILLED SHRIMP BISQUE
BROILED CHICKEN
BROCCOLI AMANDINE
GRILLED TOMATOES
PERSIAN MELON

ZUPPA DI PESCE

An Italian fish soup, with a rich, lusty sauce as a base, that is infinitely variable and can be adapted to whatever fish and seafood are available.

⅓ cup olive oil
1 onion, sliced thin
1 tablespoon chopped celery
3 cloves minced garlic
Fresh herbs, if possible:
2 or 3 sprigs marjoram
or
2 or 3 sprigs thyme
or
3 sprigs basil
Ground black pepper (no salt)

2 pounds tomatoes, diced
½ cup white wine
About 3 pounds fish and/or shellfish (mussels, shrimp, fish, a few scallops, clams)
Chopped parsley
Grated lemon peel
12 slices toasted French bread

Put the olive oil in a deep pan over medium heat. When warm add the onion. As it begins to brown, add the celery, garlic, whatever herb is being used and the pepper. Cook for a minute or two before adding the tomatoes. Add the tomatoes. When the tomatoes have stewed for 3 or 4 minutes, add the wine. Cook for several minutes more, letting it bubble a bit before turning down the heat. Cook until the tomatoes have been reduced to a pulp. Then add a cup of hot water or enough to make the mixture about the consistency of a thick soup. Let it simmer a few minutes more. This much can be done ahead. About ½ hour before serving, heat the soup; add the shellfish or fish about 10 to 12 minutes before serving. The shrimp should be peeled first, even though this is an all-four-feet-in-the-trough dish and not for the dainty. Sprinkle the soup with the parsley and grated lemon peel. Ladle into your largest soup bowls, with 3 slices of French bread in each. Be sure to have a large bowl on the table for the empty shells if the stew has mussels in it. *Serves 4.*

MENU:

ZUPPA DI PESCE
ITALIAN BREAD
MIXED GREEN SALAD
CAFFE GRANITA (Italian espresso coffee sherbet)

MOULES À LA CRÉMAILLÈRE

This is a sinfully and wondrously rich dish and is surprisingly filling. A broiled steak and satiny heads of Belgian endive are more than enough to follow. Pull the leaves off one by one with your fingers, dipping languorously in some seasoned olive oil as you eat. The bitter and elegant leaves emphasize and complement the voluptuous soup.

½ cup finely chopped shallots or green onions
⅓ cup sweet butter
¼ cup finely chopped parsley
2 cups Chablis
2 quarts mussels, well scrubbed
White pepper (no salt)
*¾ cup Hollandaise sauce**
Juice of ½ lemon

Sauté the shallots or onions in the sweet butter. Add the parsley and Chablis. Bring to a boil. Add the mussels and steam for 2 to 4 minutes or until the shells open. Remove the mussels from the broth. Pull off the top shell and discard. Strain the pan juices and stir into the Hollandaise sauce. Add the lemon juice. Stir well. Arrange the mussels on their half shells in large shallow soup plates—preferably pale celadon green—that have been warmed. Pour the sauce over them. *Serves 4.*

Hollandaise sauce—the quick blender way

Heat ½ cup of butter to bubbling, but do not brown. In blender put 3 egg yolks, 2 tablespoons of lemon juice, ¼ teaspoon salt and a pinch of cayenne. Turn motor on low speed and add hot butter gradually. Blend for about 15 seconds or until sauce is thickened and smooth. *Makes about ¾ cup.*

MENU:

MOULES À LA CRÉMAILLÈRE
FRENCH BREAD
BROILED DELMONICO STEAKS
PALE SATINY HEADS OF BELGIAN ENDIVE WITH TINY INDIVIDUAL BOWLS OF OLIVE OIL
GREENGAGE PLUM SHERBET

VENETIAN FISH SOUP

Another of the superb Italian fish soups.

3 pounds white-fleshed fish, including the heads
1 onion, studded with 2 cloves
2 bay leaves
3 sprigs parsley
1 teaspoon salt
½ teaspoon pepper
½ teaspoon dried marjoram
½ cup olive oil
1 clove garlic
½ cup dry white wine
1 cup tomatoes
Orange slices

Cut the fish from the bones and cut into bite-size pieces and save. Put the trimmings and heads in 3 cups of water with the onion, 1 bay leaf, parsley, salt, pepper and half of the marjoram. Simmer, covered, for 30 to 40 minutes. Strain and discard the clutter. Sauté the pieces of fish in the hot olive oil with the rest of the marjoram, the other bay leaf and garlic. Add the fish stock, wine and tomatoes. Simmer, covered, for about 15 minutes. Remove the garlic. Serve with a slice of orange in each bowl. *Serves 4 to 6.*

MENU:

VENETIAN FISH SOUP ITALIAN BREAD
WATERCRESS AND BEET SALAD CHOCOLATE CHEESECAKE

CIOPPINO

On the West Coast there is an infinitely varied and delectable fish and seafood catchall called cioppino. It is a lusty dish of Italian origin and somewhat related to the glorious fish mélanges of Italy. It began as most great fish dishes did with what the fishermen brought in, but has developed many precious and finicky versions.

Sauce

2 cloves garlic, minced
1 cup chopped onion
1 cup chopped green onions
1 green pepper, diced
⅓ cup olive oil
1 (1-pound, 14-ounce) can solid-packed tomatoes
1 (6-ounce) can tomato paste
1 pint clam juice
or
*1 pint fish fumet**
1 pinch thyme
1 bay leaf
1 tablespoon grated orange peel
2 cups white wine
Salt and pepper

The Fish

2 pounds fish (bass, halibut, cod), cut into pieces
18 scrubbed raw clams
1 pound peeled raw shrimp
1 cooked lobster
or
2 cooked West Coast crabs
or
4 cooked East Coast blue crabs

Sauté the garlic, onion, green onions and pepper in the oil until golden. Then add the tomatoes, tomato paste, clam juice or fumet, thyme, orange peel and bay leaf. Simmer for 1 to 2 hours until thick and unctuous. Add the wine. Arrange the cut-up fish on the bottom of a deep pot, then the cut-up pieces of crab or lobster, and top with the shrimp and clams. Add the sauce, cover and simmer for about 20 to 30 minutes or until the fish is done. Serve in large soup bowls with crescent-shaped dishes ready for bones. If your ménage does not run to finger bowls, you might do as Old Bookbinder's Restaurant in Philadelphia does now in this streamlined age. As we looked around recently to see when they were bringing finger bowls, we were startled to receive a package of Wash 'n Dri. Of course an effete version of cioppino can be made with the shellfish removed from their shells beforehand, but it does seem to spoil the fun. *Serves 6 to 8 lustily.*

MENU:

CIOPPINO
GARLIC BREAD
MIXED GREEN SALAD
WINE SHERBET AND THIN GINGER COOKIES

PRETZEL SOUP WITH CLAMS
(Bretzel Supp mit Clams)

The Pennsylvania Dutch, who usually have pretzels on hand and are superb cooks, almost invariably break pretzels into oyster stew or clam soup. And the contrast in textures and flavors is most pleasing.

1 (7-ounce) can minced clams and juice
2 cups clam juice (bottled)
2 cups milk
½ teaspoon ground thyme
½ teaspoon salt
½ clove garlic
¼ teaspoon pepper
2 teaspoons grated onion
2 tablespoons finely chopped parsley
4 tablespoons butter
2 tablespoons flour
½ cup light or heavy cream
Paprika
12 large pretzels or a proportionate amount of pretzel sticks

Drain the clams and put the juice from the clams and bottled clam juice in a saucepan with the milk, thyme, salt, garlic, pepper, onion and parsley. Simmer the mixture very gently for 5 minutes, being careful not to let it come to a boil. In another saucepan melt half the butter, stir in the flour and cook for a few minutes until well blended. Gradually stir in, a little at a time, a cup of the milk-and-clam mixture, stirring well. Add the rest. Heat and stir until slightly thickened. Add the minced clams, cream and remaining butter. Heat thoroughly. Serve sprinkled with paprika. And pass the pretzels, so that each can crumble them in his soup before eating. *Serves 6.*

MENU:

PRETZEL SOUP WITH CLAMS
HAM, ONION AND POTATO CASSEROLE
WATERCRESS SALAD CHERRY PIE

BRETON FISH SOUP

All fish soups, no matter how complicated and pretentious the recipes have become, began with what the fishermen brought home and what their wives had on hand. This one from Brittany is simple and good. It is best, of course, made with fish just pulled from the sea, but is often better with frozen fish fillets and shrimp than with some tired or indifferent market fish and shrimp. Almost any simple combination of fish or fish and shellfish can be used.

1 bunch spring onions, chopped
3 or 4 sprigs sorrel (sour grass) or chopped fresh dill
1 bunch parsley, chopped
1 bunch chives, chopped
3 or 4 sprigs mint, chopped
3 tablespoons butter
Salt and pepper
2 pounds fish fillets
½ pound peeled shrimp, or oysters

Put all of the ingredients in a gallon soup pot with the fish and 2 quarts of water and simmer for ½ hour, after bringing to boil and then reducing heat. About 10 minutes before serving add the shrimp, or oysters. *Serves 6 to 8.*

MENU:

BRETON FISH SOUP
BOILED POTATOES
FRENCH BREAD
RADISH AND WATERCRESS SALAD
RHUBARB CUSTARD TART

SELIANKA

It may be the long cold winters, when it is pleasurable to cook, that makes Russians so adept at making soups of substance—soups that "recruit the spirits," to use one of Abigail Adams' vivid phrases. This fish soup is fine with its tart emphasis somewhat allied to the Rumanian ciorbas. It is usually made with smoked salmon but the fresh can be used for a different and good flavor.

¾ pound haddock fillets, cod or other fresh or frozen white fish, cut into small squares
4 thin slices smoked salmon, cut into thin strips
2 tablespoons butter
2 tablespoons flour
2 tablespoons tomato purée
6 cups fish fumet or clam juice
2 tablespoons minced sour gherkins
1 tablespoon minced capers
½ pound cooked shelled shrimp or Chilian langostinos, chopped coarsely
1 tablespoon minced parsley
1 cup heavy cream
Salt and pepper

Poach the fresh or frozen fish in 1 cup water for 5 minutes, add the salmon and cook for 1 minute more. Drain the fish and save the cooking liquid. Melt the butter, add the flour, stirring until smooth. Add the liquid from the fish, a little at a time, stirring well until smooth and thickened. Gradually add the tomato purée, then the fish fumet or clam juice, the fish and the rest of the ingredients except for the cream, salt and pepper. Heat thoroughly before adding the cream. Add the cream and the salt and pepper but do not boil. Serve at once. *Serves 6 to 8.*

MENU:

SELIANKA
FRENCH BREAD
CAESAR SALAD
GRAPEFRUIT HALVES TOPPED WITH VANILLA ICE CREAM SPRINKLED WITH GRATED CHOCOLATE

NASSAU FISH CHOWDER

This can be made adequately and even pleasurably, if a little less flavorfully, with frozen fish fillets and clam juice.

Fishbones and trimmings
1 pound fresh halibut, boned, skinned and cut into squares
3 pounds striped bass, boned, skinned and cut into squares
Salt and pepper
4 large potatoes, diced
1 large Bermuda onion, peeled and sliced
or
6 small white onions, sliced paper-thin
1 large can peeled tomatoes
1 tablespoon mixed whole pickling spices
1 cup sherry
2 to 4 tablespoons Worcestershire sauce
Juice of 1 lime or a lemon
2 tablespoons butter

Put the fishbones, skin and trimmings (which you reminded your fish man to send you) in an enamel pan with 3 cups of cold water and simmer gently until there are about 2 cups of strong fish stock, or use some fish fumet you have frozen. Now wash the fish, drain and put in a large enamel pan. Sprinkle the diced potatoes over the fish, then lay the sliced onion on the potatoes. Pour in the tomatoes, fish stock and mixed spices. Bring slowly to a simmer and cook very slowly for 2 hours. Stir very gently from time to time, being careful not to break up the fish. Just before serving, check the seasonings and add more salt if necessary, the sherry, Worcestershire sauce and lime or lemon juice. At the very last minute add the butter and when it is melted turn into a soup tureen and serve in soup plates. *Serves 6.*

MENU:

NASSAU FISH CHOWDER
FRENCH BREAD
WATERMELON HALF FILLED WITH MIXED SMALL FRUITS

SPINACH AND CLAM SOUP

Beautiful, subtle and simple.

2 packages frozen spinach
1 cup heavy cream
1 cup light cream
2 cups clam juice
Grated nutmeg

Cook the spinach and purée in a blender. Put in a pan with the heavy cream, light cream and clam juice. Stir well and heat. Serve hot or cold sprinkled with grated nutmeg on top. *Serves 4.*

MENU:

SPINACH AND CLAM SOUP
COLD SALMON WITH DILL
SPOON BREAD
WATERCRESS WITH ROQUEFORT CHEESE DRESSING
WINE SHERBET WITH STRAWBERRIES
BLACK WALNUT COOKIES

SEA SOUP

A soup that will make the romantic ones think of the first sniff of salt water on a drive toward the ocean.

2 cups scallops	*Salt and paprika*
1 tablespoon lemon juice	*1 quart milk*
2 tablespoons butter	*Sliced lime*

Chop the scallops, sprinkle with the lemon juice and let stand for about 20 minutes. Add 1 cup of water, bring to a boil. Add the butter, salt, paprika and milk. Cook for about 8 minutes. Serve with a thin slice of lime in each small bowl. *Serves 4 to 6.*

MENU:

SEA SOUP
STUFFED BLACK BASS
RICE AND WILD RICE PILAF
BROILED TOMATOES
HONEYDEW MELON

MANHATTAN CLAM CHOWDER

While I happily inhabit the very crowded island of Manhattan, I seldom eat or serve its clam chowder. But here it is for those less prejudiced.

1 quart clams or 3 cans minced clams
¼ pound salt pork, coarsely diced
3 medium onions, chopped
2 cups chopped peeled tomatoes
or
2 cups canned tomatoes
1 cup diced carrots
1 cup chopped celery
2 tablespoons chopped parsley
1 bay leaf
¼ teaspoon thyme
2 potatoes, diced
Pepper
Pilot crackers

Cover the clams with water and steam until they open. Strain the juice from the clams through a piece of wet cheesecloth and finally chop the clams or put them through a meat grinder. If canned clams are used, drain and save the juice, too. Sauté the salt pork in a heavy pot, remove the pieces and sauté the onion in the fat. Add the tomatoes and cook for 5 minutes. Add the remaining vegetables, seasoning, clam juice and enough water to make 3 pints of liquid. Cook over very low heat for about 1½ hours. Add the clams and potatoes and cook until the potatoes are tender. Season with pepper and salt if necessary and pour into a tureen over the crumbled crackers. *Serves 6 to 8.*

MENU:

MANHATTAN CLAM CHOWDER
BROILED HAM STEAK
CORN PUDDING
LEAF LETTUCE SALAD
LEMON SHERBET

OYSTER STEW

Simple and sublime. The only thing complicated about an oyster stew is making the decision about the proportion of cream to milk and if you even want any cream and also how many oysters to allow per bowl. A happy and informal and personal survey in restaurants in Washington, D.C., showed a rather wide spread from a meager 6 to 8 oysters in a soup bowl to a blissful and crowded 18 at one of Washington's waterfront restaurants—which, alas, is no more.

1 quart half-and-half
1 quart small oysters and juice
4 tablespoons butter
Salt and pepper
½ teaspoon Worcestershire sauce
Paprika

Heat the half-and-half in a double boiler or heavy pan, being careful not to let the liquid boil. In a small saucepan heat the oysters in their juice just until the edges curl. Put the oysters and milk together, add the butter, salt, pepper and Worcestershire sauce. Sprinkle with paprika. Serve immediately. *Serves 4.*

MENU:

OYSTER STEW
ROAST BEEF
YORKSHIRE PUDDING
BROILED TOMATOES
WINE SHERBET

ELIXIR OF CLAM SOUP

Sublimely good and embarrassingly simple if you are trying to impress someone.

1 pint clam juice
½ bay leaf
½ teaspoon thyme
Pinch of cayenne
1 cup dry white wine
1 cup heavy cream
1 egg yolk, lightly beaten

Heat the clam juice with the bay leaf, thyme, cayenne and white wine slowly for 20 to 30 minutes. Remove from the heat, strain, add the cream mixed with the slightly beaten egg yolk. Return to the stove and cook over low heat until slightly thickened. Do not let boil. *Serves 4 or 5.*

MENU:

ELIXIR OF CLAM SOUP
BROILED SALMON STEAKS
TINY NEW POTATOES
SPINACH SOUFFLÉ
LEMON CURD TARTS
CELERY STARS (small stars of piecrust sprinkled with celery seed and baked)

OYSTER BISQUE

As Alice B. Toklas has said, a blender is a blessed thing in a kitchen and a joy to all soup makers. Oysters are apt to be recalcitrant about normal ways of chopping, but are easily subdued in a blender.

1 quart oysters and juice
½ medium onion, chopped
1 clove garlic, minced
2 tablespoons butter
2 cups light cream
Salt and white pepper
Dash of Tabasco sauce

Put the oysters and juice in a blender and blend for 10 to 15 seconds. Cook the onion and garlic in the butter until transparent but not brown. Add to the oyster purée in the blender and blend for 10 seconds more. Pour into a saucepan and add the cream, salt, pepper and Tabasco sauce. Heat over low heat or hot water, stirring constantly. Do not permit this to boil. *Serves 4 to 6.*

MENU:

OYSTER BISQUE SOUFFLÉ CRACKERS
ROAST BEEF WILD RICE
ASPARAGUS ORANGES GLACÉ
MACAROONS

FISH AND SEAFOOD CHOWDER

When the younger members of the family are home from school or college, it is wise to serve dishes that can be stretched at almost a moment's notice to accommodate an unscheduled guest or two.

6 large potatoes, peeled and diced
3 large onions, sliced thin
2 pounds frozen fish fillets, cut into large pieces
1 bay leaf
1½ quarts milk
Salt and pepper
1 pound peeled cooked shrimp

Simmer all ingredients except the shrimp over very low heat until the onions and potatoes are tender, adding more milk or water if necessary for a thick, stewlike consistency. Add the cooked shrimp. Heat a minute or two and serve. *Serves 4.*

MENU:

FISH AND SEAFOOD CHOWDER
POPPYSEED ROLLS
SPINACH
SALAD WITH RICED HARD-COOKED EGGS AND FRENCH DRESSING
STRAWBERRY CHEESECAKE, FROM THE FREEZER

LOBSTER BISQUE

While this is an elegant and festive beginning to a meal, it is more frugal than it sounds, because the flavor comes from both the lobster shells and the lobster meat, but the cooked lobster can be used for a salad or Newburg at another meal. The instructions, which call for cut-up live lobster, often make the timid and tender-hearted ones wince. It is possible to have your fish man cut it up for you just before you use it *if* you are living in a region where there are fish men and fresh lobster. If not, it is possible to make a variant with frozen lobster tails, which have the merit of being comfortably dead, immobile and available in most places.

1 carrot, scraped and chopped
1 onion, chopped
1 small bunch parsley, chopped
1 stalk celery, chopped
¼ cup (½ stick) butter
2 pounds live lobster, cut up
or
2 pounds lobster tails, cut up
Salt and pepper
¼ cup cognac
⅓ cup white wine
1 pound can tomatoes
4 cups chicken consommé
2 tablespoons more butter
¼ cup heavy cream
Tiny slivers of cooked lobster meat
Sherry

Sauté the vegetables in the butter for a few minutes. Add the lobster, shell and all. Simmer until the lobster is red, 15 to 20 minutes. Then add the salt, pepper, cognac and white wine. After a few minutes add the tomatoes and half of the consommé. Cook for 15 minutes, remove the lobster and reserve for another dish. Add the rest of the consommé and let the bisque boil slowly for 30 minutes. Strain, add the rest of the butter and the cream. Serve in cups and pass the sherry, so that each can add a few drops if he wishes. The slivers of lobster can be added but they're not essential. *Serves 8.*

MENU:

LOBSTER BISQUE FRENCH BREAD
BROILED LAMB CHOPS BROILED TINY NEW POTATOES
WATERCRESS AND GRAPEFRUIT SALAD BISCUIT TORTONI

5

Great Soups – Fish

In this admittedly personal and arbitrary grouping of recipes, a great soup is a main dish, and an important one that comes to mind when one thinks of a country or a region. Some that qualify are bouillabaisse, Maryland crab soup, New England clam chowder and my favorite of all fish soups and possibly of all soups—the French bourride, although it is not a main-dish soup.

MARYLAND CRAB SOUP

For anyone but Marylanders this soup is a meal in itself, but for them it is merely an overture to an orgy of steamed crabs. It is not usually a day-in-and-day-out soup that you whip up for yourself, but is one for an occasion and usually for a large number of people. Customarily it is served out of doors or at firemen's carnivals, etc. Obviously, after such a meal little else is needed. The soup is usually made in the summer when crabs and vegetables—and watermelons, too—are plentiful. Watermelons are a fresh, typical and appropriate ending. If you wish to finish such a robust meal more genteelly, serve a beautiful watermelon sherbet, sprinkled with fresh blackberries. Beer is drunk throughout the meal.

10 steamed crabs
1 pound shin beef, in 1 piece
or
1 chicken, cut up
¼ pound bacon, in 1 piece
½ teaspoon salt
6 potatoes, peeled and diced
3 tomatoes, quartered
2 onions, chopped
1 cup whole kernel corn, cut from the cob, frozen or canned
1 cup lima beans
1 cup string beans, cut into pieces
2 tablespoons sugar
3 stalks celery, chopped
1 green pepper, seeded and cut into pieces
1 cup peas
½ cup chopped parsley
2 teaspoons Worcestershire sauce

Break off the claws from the bodies of the crabs, discard the small claws and crack the large claws. Pull off the back shell, remove the gills or devil and the face of the crab (the eyes and sandbag should come off with the shell). Break the crab in half and cut across each half parallel to the shells but do not remove the meat. Put the body pieces, large claws, bacon, beef, vegetables and seasonings in a large pot with about 2 quarts of water, adding more if necessary for a consistency halfway between a soup and a stew. Simmer for 1 to 2 hours. *Serves 12 or more.*

MENU:

DEVILED EGGS
MARYLAND CRAB SOUP
STEAMED CRABS (traditional but not necessary)
CORN BREAD
WATERMELON SHERBET WITH FRESH BLACKBERRIES

BOURRIDE

The chapters in a book devoted to soups are necessarily somewhat arbitrarily arranged, which is the reason for including the bourride with great soups rather than in the chapter devoted to fish soups. To me, a French bourride is the greatest of all fish soups, although this is a contentious statement.

*Fish fumet**
4 thick fish fillets
Aioli

Prepare the fish fumet, and poach the fish fillets in it. Transfer them to warm soup bowls. Beat the fish broth into the aioli (below) with a whisk or rotary beater. Pour into the soup bowls over the fish fillets and serve immediately. *Serves 4.*

Aioli

2 cloves garlic
1 egg
½ teaspoon dry mustard
½ teaspoon salt
2 tablespoons vinegar
1 cup salad oil or part olive oil, part salad oil

Put garlic, egg, mustard, salt, vinegar and ¼ of the oil in a blender. Cover and blend at low speed. Remove the cover and pour in the remaining oil while the motor is going. When oil has all been added, the aioli is done. If you haven't a blender, add the juice from 2 cloves of garlic, squeezed in a garlic press, to 1¼ cups of commercial mayonnaise and stir well.

MENU:

GOUGÈRE
BOURRIDE
FRENCH BREAD
CHEF'S SALAD (julienne strips of green onions, Swiss cheese and prosciutto ham, Bibb lettuce with French dressing)
FRESH STRAWBERRIES WITH THEIR HULLS AND A MOUND OF POWDERED SUGAR

NEW ENGLAND CLAM CHOWDER

Once upon a time I had New England clam chowder at its celestial best. It is seldom that the ingredients are together at one time in their perfect state. Not only were the clams quivering fresh from the sea but it was a perfect summer night on the Connecticut shore, the conversation was varied and good and the hostess a superb and imaginative cook. Somewhat inexplicably there was some left-over lobster, and the butter in which other lobsters had been dipped had been saved. The cut-up lobster and lobster-flavored butter were added to the chowder. Obviously, one can't rashly give a receipt that requires leftover lobster and lobster butter, but rather consolingly I say it is difficult to make a bad clam chowder.

2 dozen clams
or
3 (10½-ounce) cans minced clams
½ pound diced lean salt pork
2 onions, diced
3 large potatoes, peeled and diced
2 cups milk
2 cups light cream
2 tablespoons butter
Salt and pepper
Pilot or common crackers

Steam the clams until open, drain and strain the clam juice and save, or drain the canned minced clams and save the juice. Add water to it if necessary to make 4 cups. Fry the salt pork in a deep saucepan, add the onion and cook slowly until a golden brown. Add the potatoes and clam juice. Bring to a boil, then turn down and simmer until the potatoes are tender. Add the milk, cream and chopped clams. Add the butter, salt and pepper and serve immediately, poured over the broken crackers. *Serves 6 to 8.*

MENU:

NEW ENGLAND CLAM CHOWDER
COMMON CRACKERS
SALAD NIÇOISE

BRAZILIAN FISH STEW

Much like fish stews elsewhere except for the emphasis of the chili pepper and lemon juice.

1 clove garlic, minced
2 tablespoons olive oil
1 small onion, sliced
4 tomatoes, peeled, seeded and diced
½ green pepper, seeded and diced
1 tablespoon minced parsley
½ bay leaf
½ can green chili pepper, chopped (about 3 hot green peppers)
6 slices fish fillets (halibut or sole)
*1 cup clam juice or fish fumet**
Juice of ½ lemon
Salt and pepper
Tabasco sauce

Brown the garlic in the olive oil in a deep skillet. Add the onion, tomatoes, green pepper, parsley, bay leaf and chili pepper. Simmer 10 minutes. Cut the fish into pieces, add the clam juice or fish fumet, lemon juice, salt and pepper. Add ½ cup of water and simmer for ½ hour or until the fish flakes. Remove the bay leaf. Add the Tabasco sauce, and salt and pepper if necessary. *Serves 4.*

MENU:

BRAZILIAN FISH STEW
SESAME SEED ROLLS
ITALIAN SALAD (cooked potatoes, pitted ripe olives and cooked crisp zucchini with French dressing)
BOYSENBERRY SHERBET

BOUILLABAISSE

The secret of a bouillabaisse is the fast cooking over a fierce fire that blends oil and stock into a smooth mixture rather than an esoteric and unprecise combination of ingredients. Any harmonious combination of fresh or frozen fish or shellfish will do, and the fresher the better. There are different ways of serving it. In the traditional way, the fish and shellfish are arranged on a hot platter and the broth strained into a tureen. Thin pieces of French bread are placed in each soup plate. Add an assortment of shellfish and cover with the broth. Some pass freshly grated Parmesan cheese, but that is *not* traditional. Neither is serving the pieces of seafood in the tureen with the strained broth, but it is simple if there is not much room on the table, and it looks like "a real rich dish," as a tongue-in-cheek friend says.

⅓ cup olive oil
2 leeks, chopped
2 onions, chopped
2 cloves garlic, minced
3 tomatoes, peeled, seeded and diced
½ teaspoon thyme
¼ teaspoon rosemary
1 teaspoon grated orange peel
⅛ teaspoon saffron
Salt and pepper
*1 pint fish fumet**
or
1 pint clam juice
1 cup white wine
4 to 5 pounds fish and shellfish (fish fillets, shrimp, scallops, lobster, etc.), cut into serving-size pieces
Finely chopped parsley

In a large kettle or pot, heat the oil, add the leeks, onion and garlic and cook for about 5 minutes. Add the tomatoes, seasonings, fish fumet and wine. Simmer for 15 minutes. Bring to a fast boil, add the fish and shellfish and boil for 15 minutes. Transfer the seafood to a hot platter or tureen. Strain the broth and pour into the tureen. Sprinkle with parsley. *Serves 6 to 8.*

MENU:

MELON WITH PROSCIUTTO
BOUILLABAISSE
FRENCH BREAD
BIBB LETTUCE SALAD WITH LEMON DRESSING
WINE SHERBET

HAM AND OYSTER GUMBO

In and around New Orleans a gumbo can be made with almost any pleasing combination of chicken, ham, seafood and assorted vegetables. To be authentic and give it its wondrously slippery consistency, it must have either okra or filé powder, and many versions have both. The filé powder is never cooked but is added after the gumbo is removed from the heat.

3 slices bacon, diced
1 cup chopped onion
1 clove chopped garlic
1 pound diced raw ham
1 can (1 pound) tomatoes
2 cups clam juice
1 package frozen okra or 1 pint fresh
1 pint frozen or fresh oysters
1 teaspoon filé powder
Salt and pepper
Tabasco sauce
Cooked rice

Cook the bacon over low heat with the onion and garlic until pale yellow but not brown. Add the diced ham, tomatoes, clam juice and okra. Simmer until the ham and okra are tender. Add the oysters and their juice. Simmer until the edges curl. Remove from the heat, add the filé powder, salt, pepper and a very cautious dash of Tabasco sauce. Ladle into soup bowls, pass the bowl of cooked rice for each to spoon into his bowl of gumbo. A tablespoon of rice to a bowl of gumbo is the usual proportion. Eat the French-fried eggplant as a finger food with the gumbo instead of the very good and traditional French bread. *Serves 4.*

MENU:

HAM AND OYSTER GUMBO
FRENCH-FRIED EGGPLANT
DICED CUCUMBER WITH CHOPPED FRESH MINT AND YOGHURT
HOT RASPBERRY TURNOVER

SHRIMP GUMBO

A superb meal-in-itself soup.

¼ cup flour
1 cup green onions, with tops and bottoms, chopped
4 tablespoons bacon drippings or butter
2 (8-ounce) bottles clam juice
1 large can Italian plum tomatoes, drained
1 bay leaf
1 teaspoon Worcestershire sauce
¼ teaspoon thyme
Salt
½ teaspoon sugar
Freshly ground black pepper
2 pounds raw shrimp, peeled and deveined
1 package frozen okra
1 teaspoon grated lemon peel
½ teaspoon filé powder
Chopped parsley
Hot cooked rice

Brown the flour in a dry skillet, stirring. Cook the onion in the bacon drippings or butter in a deep pot until the onion becomes translucent, about 5 minutes. Sprinkle the browned flour over them and stir in the clam juice. Cook over low heat, stirring constantly, until smooth and thickened. Add the tomatoes, bay leaf, Worcestershire sauce, seasonings, except for the filé powder, and shrimp. Cook for about 10 minutes or more, add the okra and stir until the pieces are separated. Cook the okra for 10 to 15 minutes or until tender but still crisp. Remove from the heat, add the filé powder and put in a tureen. Serve in soup bowls with a spoonful of rice and parsley sprinkled on top. (Filé powder can be found in food specialty shops. It must never be cooked but is added at the last minute.) *Serves 4 to 6.*

MENU:

HOT ROASTED PORK CUBES
SHRIMP GUMBO
HOT ROLLS
RAW SPINACH SALAD WITH HOT BACON DRESSING
BOWL OF BLUE, RED AND WHITE GRAPES

LOBSTER STEW

A lobster stew made from live lobsters is a very great stew in its flavors and simplicity. There is no need to gild the lily—or rather, the lobster. The lobster meat colors the stew with its own pink. It is best if made ahead of time and allowed to stand in the refrigerator overnight and then reheated. The only trick is to stir constantly while the milk is being added so that it does not curdle.

3 live lobsters (1½ to 2 pounds each)
or
1 live lobster (5½ to 6 pounds)
¼ pound (1 stick) butter
2 quarts milk
No salt or pepper

Cook the lobsters in 5 or 6 quarts of rapidly boiling water in a large kettle, using one tablespoon of salt for each quart of water. Cover and boil for 7 to 10 minutes per pound for the smaller lobsters, or 30 to 35 minutes in all for the large one. Remove from the water and cool enough to handle. Remove the intestinal vein that goes the length of the tail and back; save everything else, especially the green tomalley (liver) and pink coral. Simmer the liver and tomalley in the butter in a very heavy pot for 7 or 8 minutes, and then add the lobster meat cut into fairly big pieces. Cook it about 4 minutes, turn the heat down and add the milk slowly, stirring constantly until the milk bubbles around the edges. Let cool and then refrigerate overnight. The next day reheat before serving. *Serves 4.*

MENU:

PIGS IN BLANKETS
LOBSTER STEW
COMMON CRACKERS
BELGIUM ENDIVE
STRAWBERRY SHORTCAKE MADE FROM DROP BISCUIT

FLORIDA KEY CONCH CHOWDER

The rich and sophisticated and the poor eat many of the same dishes. Some of the best are those such as this, which the timid and safe and conservative often overlook.

4 conchs (removed from shells)
¼ pound salt pork, diced
2 cloves garlic
1 small onion, chopped
1 stalk celery, minced
Salt and pepper
¼ teaspoon thyme
1 bay leaf
½ teaspoon oregano
2 cups canned tomatoes
2 cups diced potatoes
2 sweet peppers, chopped
Extra tomato juice
Sherry

Soak the conchs in salt water for ½ hour, drain and place on a wooden board and pound to tenderize. They can be tenderized in a pressure cooker efficiently and untraditionally by cooking with 1 cup of water for 35 minutes at 15 pounds pressure. The Italians, who call conchs scungilli, sell them canned as well as fresh and cook them much the same way. Fry the salt pork till crisp and remove from the fat. Sauté the garlic, onion and celery in the pork fat. Add the conchs, salt, pepper, thyme, bay leaf and oregano. Cover with water and simmer for about 2½ hours until the conchs are tender. Add the tomatoes, potatoes and peppers. Add more tomato juice or water if necessary for a sloshy consistency. Cook till vegetables are tender. Add sherry to taste. *Serves 4.*

MENU:

FLORIDA KEY CONCH CHOWDER

SAFFRON RICE

CUBAN BREAD

LEMON CURD TARTS

6

Great Soups – Meat

Many of the truly great soups are a production, in the theatrical sense, in their making and their presentation. Sometimes the broth is served separately, then the vegetables and sliced meat as in the French pot-au-feu, the Spanish olla podrida or the Algerian couscous.

BIGOS

What is said to have started out as a hunter's stew in Poland has become a dish much admired in many cuisines, including the American. Even those who think they do not like sauerkraut except on hot dogs invariably change their minds after tasting some of the superb European stews such as this. The flavor of sauerkraut is excitingly blended and subtly muted by long cooking with other ingredients. This is better if cooked a day or so ahead and reheated.

2 pounds sauerkraut
¼ cup sliced dried mushrooms
2 medium sweet apples, peeled, cored and sliced
1 (20-ounce) can tomatoes
10 peppercorns
1 tablespoon sugar
2 tablespoons prepared mustard
1 bay leaf
2 cups diced Polish sausage or frankfurters or leftover meat such as beef, veal, pork or lamb
1 cup diced salt pork or bacon

Rinse the sauerkraut with cold water and squeeze dry. Soak the dried mushrooms for several hours in water to cover. Bring to a boil and simmer until tender. Add with cooking liquid to the sauerkraut. Add the apples, tomatoes and seasonings. Cover and simmer for 1¼ hours. Add the diced meat and salt pork to the sauerkraut. Cook for 1 hour longer. Serve with steamed potatoes on the side. *Serves 4 to 6.*

MENU:

CLAM PANCAKES
BIGOS
STEAMED POTATOES
FRENCH BREAD
STRAWBERRY CHEESECAKE

POT-AU-FEU

A pot-au-feu is a way of life almost more than a soup. Customarily the broth is eaten first and then the sliced meat and vegetables are served on a platter as the next course. Other times and untraditionally the beef is sliced and served with the broth and vegetables in the soup bowls. Often leftover beef is made into a salad and served the following day.

2 pounds beef shank with meat
Extra beef bones
6 chicken backs
1 turnip, cut up
3 leeks, trimmed and washed
1 large onion, quartered but not peeled
3 tablespoons tomato ketchup
Juice of ½ lemon
1 tablespoon celery seed
1 teaspoon dried rosemary
2 cloves garlic, chopped
3 or 4 whole cloves
3 to 4 pounds beef, round or rump, in a chunk
1 whole chicken (for a lavish touch but not obligatory)
1 veal or calf's tongue (for another lavish touch but not obligatory)
4 cans beef consommé
1 cup diced carrots
1 cup Italian green beans
2 cups diced potatoes
1 cup shelled peas

In a deep 2-gallon soup pot put the beef shank, extra beef bones, chicken backs, turnip, leeks, onion, ketchup, lemon juice, celery seed, rosemary, garlic, cloves, beef in a chunk and the whole chicken and calf's tongue if used. Add the beef consommé and water enough to cover all the ingredients. Cover and bring to a boil, skimming off the scum as it appears. When it is boiling merrily, turn the heat down to a simmer and cook for 4 to 5 hours. Remove the chunk of meat, chicken and tongue and put aside for the next day. Remove the kettle from the heat and when cool enough to manage, strain the mixture through a colander into another kettle and throw away the tired vegetables, and do the same with the bones or give them to the dog. Refrigerate the broth until the next day. Remove the broth from the refrigerator and carefully lift the fat from the top. Put the greaseless soup in a kettle and add to it the chunk of beef, carrots, beans, potatoes (and the chicken and tongue if you are having the lavish version). After ½ hour of simmering, add the peas just long enough to barely cook them. When it is done, transfer the meat to a warm platter and slice as you would a pot roast. Pour the soup itself with its vegetables into a tureen. Serve at the table, ladling into large soup plates. Pass the sliced beef (and chicken and tongue if they were included). Serve with fresh radishes, sour pickles, coarse salt and Sauce Gribiche* on the side.

Sauce Gribiche

1 egg yolk
Salt and freshly ground black pepper to taste
1 teaspoon prepared mustard, preferably Dijon or Dusseldorf
3 tablespoons wine vinegar
½ cup olive oil
½ cup vegetable oil
2 tablespoons finely chopped shallot
1 tablespoon finely chopped onion
¼ teaspoon thyme
3 tablespoons chopped chives
¼ cup finely chopped parsley
1 teaspoon finely chopped fresh tarragon or ½ teaspoon dried tarragon
1 hard-cooked egg, sieved or finely chopped
¼ cup cold water (approximately)

Make the sauce as you make a mayonnaise. Place the egg yolk in a mixing bowl and add the salt, pepper, mustard and vinegar. Immediately begin whipping the mixture with a wire whisk or rotary beater. Add the oil, a few drops at a time; then continue adding in a steady stream, beating constantly. The sauce should become increasingly thick. Stir in the remaining ingredients, adding only enough water to the mixture to make a thin sauce. *Makes about 2 cups.*

MENU:

COLD TOMATO HALVES WITH SCRAMBLED EGGS
POT-AU-FEU
FRENCH BREAD
GREEN SALAD

RUMANIAN CIORBA WITH MEATBALLS

The national soup, as it were, of Rumania is the ciorba, which can be made with almost all meats, all fish and even vegetables. It is sour and is better when cooked a day or two ahead. In Rumania it is soured by fermented wheat bran, unripened green grapes, green plums, sorrel leaves and sauerkraut juice. Lemons, which can also be used, are a luxury touch there. In our affluent society sauerkraut juice and lemons are the easiest to come by and the easiest to use.

Broth

Veal shank bone
Pork bones from pork chops (see Meatballs)*
2 large carrots, cut in half lengthwise
1 rib celery with leaves, chopped
1 tomato, quartered
⅓ cup parsley clusters
Salt and pepper
1 quart sauerkraut juice

Meatballs

½ pound veal
½ pound pork (cut from ¾ pound of pork chops)
1 egg
Salt and pepper
1 tablespoon finely chopped parsley
1 small onion, finely chopped
¼ teaspoon thyme
2 tablespoons rice
Flour

Finish

2 tablespoons uncooked rice
1 stalk celery, chopped
1 pound leeks, cut into inch pieces
1 knob fennel, cut into pieces, with part of the green top minced
½ teaspoon thyme
⅓ cup chopped parsley
2 or 3 tarragon sprigs
A piece of hot red pepper pod
1 cup sour cream and some for topping
2 egg yolks, slightly beaten
1 tablespoon flour
1 tablespoon chopped fresh dill
or
½ teaspoon dill weed

In a large pot put the veal shank and pork bones with 3 quarts of water. Bring to a boil, add the carrots, celery, tomato and parsley. Cover and boil until the vegetables are tender. Pour in the sauerkraut juice, bring again to a boil. Cover and let stand with the heat off while preparing the meatballs.

Grind together the veal and pork, which has been cut from the chops, with a fine blade. This is better done in your home meat grinder than at the butcher's because there other bits of meat get mixed in. Mix with the whole egg, salt, pepper, parsley, onion, thyme and rice (which has been rinsed in cold water). Mix thoroughly with your hands and form into small balls the size of walnuts. Roll the meatballs in flour and let stand on a chopping board.

Strain the soup into another pot and taste for sourness. The soup is supposed to be rather sour, but it can be made less so by diluting with water, or more so by adding a little more sauerkraut juice. Bring to a boil and add 2 more tablespoons of rice rinsed in cold water. When the boiling begins, drop in the meatballs, chopped celery, leeks, fennel, thyme, parsley, tarragon and the piece of hot pepper pod. Mix the sour cream in a bowl with the slightly beaten egg yolks and flour and add a little cold water until you have a thin paste. Pour this into the ciorba, stirring constantly. Let boil slowly for 20 minutes with the pot covered to keep in the wonderful aroma. If possible, cool and let ripen in the refrigerator for 1 to 2 days, or freeze. Reheat and serve with a tablespoon of sour cream and fresh dill or tarragon on each bowl. On the side serve chopped red or green hot pepper. This is a large amount because a ciorba improves with time. The flavor keeps reacting and penetrating into the ingredients. It must be kept tightly covered in the refrigerator and can be frozen in pint plastic containers for the underprivileged small families who would otherwise have to forgo this exciting and aromatic treat. As Alice B. Toklas has said, who knows how many this will serve; it depends on how much you like it. *Serves 6 to 8 generously in large soup bowls or makes several meals for smaller numbers.*

MENU:

RUMANIAN CIORBA WITH MEATBALLS
ANADAMA BREAD
COCONUT CUSTARD PIE

COCIDO

A cocido is much like a French pot-au-feu but of course with a Spanish flavor. It varies from cook to cook and according to the circumstances. For lavish occasions uncooked ham, a blood sausage (available in groceries selling foreign foods) and half a chicken are added. The strained broth flavored with saffron is served with a spoonful of cooked rice. The second course is often the garbanzos, accompanied by a vegetable cooked separately and dressed with hot olive oil flavored with garlic. The meat course is served last, with all the meats arranged on a platter. A bowl of tomato sauce is passed around for those who want it. It is possible to serve this in a simpler and more informal fashion all at once from a tureen or great casserole. If done this way, the meat should be sliced before transferring to a tureen or casserole. The Argentine version called puchero includes yellow squash or zucchini and fresh corn on the cob but cut into small pieces.

1 pound good stew meat, in 1 piece
¼ pound bacon, in 1 piece
1 chorizo (highly seasoned Spanish sausage available in Spanish or Mexican groceries)
1 soupbone with marrow
1 pound chick-peas or garbanzos or ceci (all the same thing), soaked overnight
4 or 5 large potatoes, peeled
Saffron
Salt and pepper

For the lavish version

½ pound uncooked ham, in 1 piece
1 blood sausage, in 1 piece
½ chicken, in 1 piece

Sauce

5 medium tomatoes, quartered
2 fat cloves garlic
½ teaspoon cumin seed
1 teaspoon oregano
2 tablespoons olive oil
Cooked rice for the broth
Cooked green vegetables (string beans, cabbage, spinach)

Wash the meat with hot water, put in a pot with boiling water and bring to a boil. Skim off the foam and turn the heat down so the pot barely simmers. After 45 minutes, add the soaked chick-peas, which have been rinsed with hot water, simmer for about 3 hours or till the garbanzos are tender. This will vary according to the age of the garbanzos and it is impossible to tell until they are cooked. Sometimes it is much simpler to use the drained canned ones. About an hour before serving, add the potatoes and salt to taste. For the sauce, simmer the tomatoes, garlic, cumin seed, and oregano in the olive oil until thick and smooth at least 45 minutes to an hour, strain and serve separately. *Serves 6 to 8.*

MENU:

BLACK OLIVES WRAPPED IN BACON AND BROILED
COCIDO
FRENCH BREAD
PINEAPPLE CHUNKS WITH FRESH OR FROZEN BLUEBERRIES

MINESTRONE GENOVESE

There are many many versions of minestrone and most are good. Italians are even less stereotyped about their cooking then others. The favorite of many is the Genovese version with pesto. Pesto is an especially delectable blend of garlic, fresh basil leaves, grated Parmesan or pecorino cheese and olive oil. Other times it is used to dress pasta or spread on Italian bread. When fresh basil is available, the pesto can be prepared and frozen for future use.

1 pound of beef cut in chunks, if you wish
½ small cabbage, shredded
⅓ cup green beans
⅓ cup shelled fresh peas
3 stalks celery, diced
3 small potatoes, diced
1 cup dried beans (kidney, cranberry, ceci or so on), soaked and cooked
¼ cup olive oil
2 teaspoons salt
1 cup ditali or elbow macaroni

Put the meat and vegetables in a pan with the cooked dried beans, 3 quarts of water, olive oil and salt. Cook until the vegetables are soft and the liquid reduced. About 10 minutes before serving, add the pasta. *Serves 4 to 6.*

Pesto

2 cloves garlic
½ cup basil leaves
½ cup grated Parmesan, Sardo or pecorino cheese
½ cup olive oil

Chop the garlic and basil together until very fine, add the grated cheese and then the olive oil and mix to a paste. This can be done with a mortar pestle. This is prepared ahead and kept in the refrigerator or freezer until just before adding to the soup. *Makes about 1 cup.*

MENU:

MINESTRONE GENOVESE
SLICED ORANGE AND ONION SALAD WITH WATERCRESS, BLACK OLIVES AND FRENCH DRESSING
GARLIC BREAD
BANANA ICE CREAM
BLACK WALNUT COOKIES

BURGOO

A burgoo is basically a highly exaggerated and fancified version of a Brunswick stew. It is served on special occasions, usually in Kentucky on Derby Day. It does vary, of course, but mostly there are lots of meats and lots of vegetables cooked for a long time until they become wondrously and odorously intermingled in the soup.

2 pounds beef shank
1 pound salt pork, diced
2 pounds veal shank
2 pounds lamb breast
4 pounds chicken
2 cups chopped onion
4 cups diced potatoes
4 cups tomato purée
2 cups lima beans
1 cup diced celery
2 cups sliced okra
2 cups whole fresh corn cut from the cob or frozen niblet corn
1 cup chopped green pepper
5 bay leaves
Tabasco sauce
Worcestershire sauce to taste
1 cup chopped parsley

Put all the meat into a large kettle with 8 quarts of water and bring to a boil. Turn the heat down and simmer until the meat is tender enough to fall from the bones. Remove from the liquid, cool and remove the bones. Cut the meat into fairly large pieces. Return to the liquid, add the onion, potatoes and other vegetables and simmer until thick. Do not season until almost done, because as the stew cooks down, the seasonings become stronger. Worcestershire sauce should be added until the mixture is highly seasoned. Add the chopped parsley just before serving. This takes about 10 hours. The meat is usually cooked one day and the vegetables added and the cooking finished the next day. It should be thick but still soupy. *Obviously this serves a large group, and it is difficult to say exactly how many, but at least 12 and possibly many more.*

MENU:

HOT CHEESE BALLS BURGOO HOT BISCUITS
FRESH PINEAPPLE CHUNKS WITH FRESH RASPBERRIES SPRINKLED WITH FINELY CHOPPED CANDIED ORANGE PEEL AND SOUR CREAM

COUSCOUS

In North Africa couscous is the national dish, as it almost is in the student quarter of Paris. It is made with the couscous cereal, which is a finely ground semolina. Like many of the other big national dishes, such as pot-au-feu, it's half soup and half stew. Sometimes the couscous is served on a platter, the meat and vegetables on top, and the liquid passed separately in a pitcher. Other times it is served in a bowl as soup. Nothing dreadful happens even when barley or cracked wheat or kasha is used in place of the hard-to-find couscous.

1 large can chick-peas
2 pounds lamb, mutton or beef, cut into serving-size pieces
1 tablespoon olive oil
2 tablespoons butter
¾ cup finely chopped onion
2 teaspoons salt
½ teaspoon freshly ground pepper
⅛ teaspoon red pepper
½ teaspoon turmeric
2 tablespoons tomato paste
2 knucklebones
3 cups diced potatoes
2 cups coarsely diced yellow or white squash
2 cups coarsely diced zucchini
*Stock**
1 pound semolina, cracked wheat or kasha
2 tablespoons orange flower water
¼ teaspoon cinnamon
¼ teaspoon cloves
2 hard-cooked eggs, cut in eighths

Drain the chick-peas. Brown the meat lightly in the olive oil and butter for about 10 minutes. While browning add the onion. When the onion is translucent, add the salt, pepper, red pepper, turmeric and tomato paste. Reduce heat and barely simmer this thick mixture for about 10 minutes more. Put in a heavy pot with the knucklebones and enough water to cover. Simmer covered until the meat can be pierced with a fork but still offers slight resistance. Add the potatoes, yellow or white squash and zucchini as well as the drained canned chick-peas. Add the stock, if necessary. Simmer, covered, until the meat and vegetables are tender, about 45 minutes longer. Remove from the heat and reserve this meat and vegetable mixture. When the fat rises to the top, skim and save 2 tablespoons of it. Rinse the semolina, cracked wheat or kasha briefly and place in the top of a perforated steamer or a couscous pot. Steam the cereal, uncovered, for 15 minutes, timing after you see steam rising from the top. Meanwhile reheat the meat and vegetable mixture. Drain the liquid and save. Remove the cereal from the steamer and add the orange flower water, cinnamon and cloves. Toss the seasoned couscous lightly in the 2 tablespoons of fat, saved from the meat mixture, and put it in a serving dish. Pour 1 cup of the drained liquid over it. Put the meat, vegetables and chick-peas on top of the couscous. Arrange the hard-cooked eggs around the platter. Use the remaining liquid as a separate sauce if you like. Serve at once. *Serves 6.*

MENU:

COUSCOUS
PIDEH (flat Near Eastern bread)
FRESH PEARS

SAUERBRATEN

A German stew with a sweet and sour sauce that begins with long marinating. Traditionally it is served with superb fluffy potato dumplings with diced bread cubes within called kartoffelklosse.

1 cup beef bouillon
2 cups red wine vinegar
½ tablespoon peppercorns
3 whole cloves
2 bay leaves
2 cloves garlic, cut in half
2 medium onions, sliced
2 tablespoons dry English mustard
¼ cup sugar
5 to 6 pounds bottom chunk or rump round roast of beef (larded if you have a willing butcher)
3 tablespoons bacon drippings
⅓ cup flour
1 cup sour cream

Simmer the bouillon and vinegar, with 1 cup of water and the seasonings. Put the meat in a deep bowl or earthen crock and pour the marinade or liquid over it. Let the meat stand in the marinade under refrigeration for at least 24 hours and preferably 3 days. Some like to let it stand even longer. Remove the meat from the marinade and pat dry. Brown in the fat in a heavy skillet or Dutch oven. Add the marinade, cover and cook in a 300° oven for 2 to 3 hours or until the meat is tender. Add more liquid, water or bouillon, if necessary. Transfer the meat to a hot deep platter and keep warm. Strain the cooking liquid and thicken with flour mixed with water to a thin paste. Stir in the sour cream. Slice the meat and pour the gravy over it. Serve the kartoffelklosse in butter in a separate bowl. *Serves 4 to 6.*

Kartoffelklosse

6 medium potatoes, boiled in their skins, peeled and riced
2 eggs, beaten
Salt
Nutmeg
½ cup flour or more
1 slice bread, diced, with crust removed
2 tablespoons butter
½ cup more of butter
¼ cup dried bread crumbs
½ cup chopped parsley

Mix the riced potatoes with the beaten eggs, salt, a sprinkling of nutmeg and the flour until the mixture sticks together. Make into balls about 1 inch in diameter. Sauté the bread cubes in the 2 tablespoons of butter until lightly browned. Poke 1 or 2 of the cubes into the center of each potato ball. Drop the balls a few at a time into 2 quarts of salted boiling water. Cook gently for about 3 to 4 minutes after they come to the surface. Remove from the liquid and cut one of them open. If the center is dried, they are sufficiently cooked. If cooked too long, the ball will fall apart and become soggy. Melt the half cup of butter, add the bread crumbs and parsley. Mix thoroughly and pour over the dumplings.

MENU:

SAUERBRATEN WITH KARTOFFELKLOSSE

BEET AND ENDIVE SALAD   APRICOT SOUFFLÉ

PHILADELPHIA PEPPER POT

People are seldom undecided about pepper pot, either they like it very much or they don't. It is highly seasoned, and one must spend many blissful hours preparing it.

2 pounds honeycomb tripe
2 pounds veal knuckle, cut in halves (have your butcher do it)
½ teaspoon dill weed
10 whole cloves
1 tablespoon crushed peppercorns
¼ teaspoon marjoram
¼ teaspoon thyme
3 medium onions
2 green peppers, chopped
4 medium potatoes, peeled and cut into cubes
3 tablespoons butter
Salt
1 small bunch parsley, chopped

Wash the tripe thoroughly, put in pot with a gallon of water. Simmer for 7 to 8 hours or until tripe is soft. Drain often. Cut into squares. Place the veal knuckle in another pot with 3 quarts of water, heat slowly, let boil for 10 minutes, skim the foam off, cover and simmer gently for 2 hours. Add the dill weed, cloves, peppercorns, marjoram and thyme and continue simmering for 1 hour. Remove the veal knuckle, cut the meat from the bone and discard the bone. Strain the liquid. Put back in a clean pot with the veal. Sauté the vegetables, onion, green pepper and potatoes in butter. Add to the soup and cook until the potatoes are tender. Salt to taste. Serve very hot with parsley sprinkled on top. *Serves 6 to 8.*

MENU:

SLICED SMOKED SALMON ON THIN PUMPERNICKEL
PHILADELPHIA PEPPER POT
HOT ROLLS
CHICORY SALAD WITH DILL DRESSING
COFFEE ICE CREAM

BELGIAN HOCHEPOT

The Belgian version of pot-au-feu usually contains pigs' feet and pigtails, which seldom appeal to Americans and are often difficult to come by except in large cities or in small groceries and butcher shops that cater to the very poor. Belgians serve the broth first separately, as do the French and the Spanish, but serve it at the same time as the meat and vegetables.

1½ pounds beef brisket
1½ pounds lamb shoulder
1½ pounds veal shoulder
3 carrots, scraped and chopped
4 leeks, peeled and chopped
2 small turnips, chopped
3 celery stalks, chopped
12 small white onions, peeled
1 small head green cabbage, quartered
Salt and pepper
1 bay leaf
8 sprigs parsley
1 sprig thyme or ½ teaspoon dried thyme
12 small chipolata sausages (2 for each person)
or
1 pound hard sausage, cut into pieces
Coarse or kosher salt

Put the brisket, lamb and veal in a large deep pot, preferably the earthenware kind called a marmite. Cover with cold water. Bring very slowly to a boil and skim thoroughly. When the scum stops rising and the stock is clear, add the vegetables and season. Cover and simmer gently for 3 hours. If using the hard sausage, put it in with the other meats at the beginning. The soft sausages are added in the last hour of cooking. When ready to serve, put the meat and sausages in the center of a hot platter. Drain the vegetables and arrange around the meat. Strain the broth, pouring a little over the meat to keep it moist. Serve the broth in a soup tureen with a side dish of very coarse salt. The broth is served at the same time as the meats and vegetables. *Serves 6.*

MENU:

BELGIAN HOCHEPOT FRENCH BREAD

DUTCH PEA SOUP

This is first cousin to the Swedish and the Danish pea soup and the Canadian habitant soup. All are lusty and sustaining soups, better cooked one day and eaten the next. The Dutch pea soup is diluted with enough water on the second day to give everyone a cup, and chopped parsley is added with fried croutons. It is then called green soup.

3 cups green split peas
2 pigs' feet
1 pound fresh bacon, in 1 piece
3 leeks, diced, white part only
2 onions, diced
1 celery root or celeriac, peeled and diced
1 cup diced celery
½ bay leaf
Salt and pepper
½ pound frankfurters, sliced
2 tablespoons butter
2 tablespoons chopped parsley

Put the split peas in a large kettle with the pigs' feet, bacon, leeks, onion, celery root and celery. Add 2½ cups of cold water and the bay leaf, cover and bring to a boil. Turn the heat down and skim the foam from the top. Simmer gently for 2 hours or until the meat on the pigs' feet separates from the bones. Discard the bones. Remove the meat, dice and save. Strain the soup and put the vegetables through a sieve or food mill or purée in a blender. Put the meat and puréed vegetables in the soup kettle. Check the seasonings, add the sliced frankfurters and butter and simmer for 5 minutes longer. Serve very hot. Sprinkle each bowl with chopped parsley. *Serves 6 to 8.*

MENU:

CELERY STUFFED WITH RED CAVIAR
DUTCH PEA SOUP
BROILED TOMATOES
DARK PUMPERNICKEL
HONEYDEW MELON SPRINKLED WITH GROUND GINGER

CARBONNADE

A classic Belgian beef stew cooked with beer, which gives it a distinctive flavor.

Flour
Salt and freshly ground black pepper
1 clove garlic, finely chopped
6 medium onions, sliced
3 tablespoons bacon fat
2 pounds boneless beef, either rump or chuck, cut into 2-inch cubes
1 (12-ounce) bottle or can beer
1 tablespoon chopped parsley
1 bay leaf
¼ teaspoon thyme
Boiled potatoes

Put the flour, salt and pepper on a platter or in a paper bag and dust the pieces of meat thoroughly. Cook the onion slices and garlic in the bacon fat, until opaque and wilted but not brown. Remove the onion from the skillet with a slotted spoon. Add the meat and brown on all sides, adding more bacon fat if necessary. Add the cooked onion to the meat and the beer, parsley, bay leaf and thyme. Cover and cook over low heat until the meat is tender, about 1¼ hours. Serve hot with boiled potatoes. *Serves 6 to 8.*

MENU:

CARBONNADE
HOT ROLLS
SLICED TOMATOES WITH FRENCH DRESSING AND CHOPPED FRESH BASIL
GREENGAGE PLUM SHERBET
MACAROONS

UKRAINIAN BORSCHT

All borschts are wonderful and lusty soups that vary from region to region and from cook to cook. The Ukrainian version has sausage along with the beef, and the better the sausage, the better the borscht. The Polish kielbasa, widely available in supermarkets and food specialty stores, has a rich flavor, but Canadian bacon can be used, also frankfurters, chipolatas or either the sweet or hot Italian sausage. The Italian sausages should be sautéed slightly, before they are added to the soup, to get rid of the excess fat.

2 pounds soup beef with cracked soupbone
1 pound lean fresh pork
½ pound smoked pork
1 bay leaf
10 peppercorns
1 clove garlic, crushed
Few sprigs parsley
1 carrot, sliced
1 stalk celery, sliced
1 leek, sliced
1 (1-pound, 14-ounce) can beets
or
8 medium beets
½ green cabbage, chopped
2 large tomatoes, peeled and quartered
2 large onions, quartered
2 tablespoons vinegar
2 teaspoons sugar
½ cup cooked or canned navy beans
1 kielbasa (Polish sausage)
or
5 frankfurters, sliced thick
Salt

Put the beef, bone and 2½ quarts of water in a kettle. Cover and bring to a boil. Simmer for 1 hour. Add the pork, bay leaf, peppercorns, garlic, parsley, carrot, celery and leek. Cover and bring to a boil. Simmer for 2 hours. If using fresh beets, put the beets except for one in a pan with boiling water to cover. Simmer, covered, for 1 hour. Peel and cut into eighths. Remove all the meat from the pot and save. Strain the broth and discard the tired vegetables. Skim off the excess fat. (This is easily done if the broth is refrigerated overnight.) Return the broth to the kettle with the cooked fresh beets (or the canned ones with their juice), kielbasa, if used, cabbage, tomatoes, onions, vinegar and sugar. Cover and cook for 30 minutes. Add the beans and frankfurters. Cook for 10 minutes. Slice the meat. Add to the soup with the one raw beet, peeled and grated. Obviously, if the canned beets are used, this step is omitted. Reheat to boiling. Season with salt. *Serves 10 to 12 lavishly.*

MENU:

UKRAINIAN BORSCHT
PIROSHKI*
FRESH FRUIT

VENISON STEW

With more leisure for almost everyone, game hunting is on the increase. The season begins about the time it gets too cold and rough for boating. Even if there is no hunter in your own family, you are apt to have a neighbor who insists on giving you samples of his prowess. The game can be kept in the freezer, but states have different laws about how much you are permitted to have on hand at one time. Venison tastes much like beef but needs gentle and moist cooking. If it is marinated in wine overnight, the flavor is improved and the meat is more tender.

2 pounds venison, cut into 1½-inch cubes
1 large onion, sliced
2 cloves garlic, chopped
1 lemon, sliced thin
3 cups beef bouillon
1 cup red wine
½ teaspoon oregano
Flour
Bacon drippings
1 bunch celery, cut into 1-inch pieces
or
1 pound celeriac, peeled and diced
10 small white onions
1 tablespoon Worcestershire sauce
1 can Italian tomato paste

Marinate the venison overnight with the onion, garlic, lemon, bouillon, red wine and oregano. The next day, remove from the marinade, pat dry, flour and sauté in bacon drippings in a skillet. Transfer to a deep pot, add the marinade, celery or celeriac and white onions. Cover, bring to a boil, turn the heat down and simmer for 1½ to 2 hours, or until tender. Add the Worcestershire sauce and tomato paste for the last ½ hour of cooking. Thicken the juices, if desired, with 2 tablespoons of flour and water mixed to a thin paste. *Serves 4 to 6.*

MENU:

KUMQUATS STUFFED WITH CREAM CHEESE
VENISON STEW
FRENCH BREAD
RED CABBAGE SLAW WITH ROQUEFORT AND SOUR CREAM DRESSING
A PITCHER OF WHOLE SKINNED PEACHES IN RED WINE (Wine is served during the meal; peaches served for dessert)

BEEF, MUSHROOM AND BARLEY SOUP

This is one of the simplest and the best. For it you need the dried black mushrooms which are sometimes Chinese and sometimes Italian in origin. The fresh ones on the market or the canned ones do not have enough flavor for this soup.

2 pounds stewing beef, cut into chunks
2 pounds beef bones
or
2 tablespoons seasoned beef base
½ teaspoon mixed pickling spice
1 lemon, sliced thin
1 teaspoon salt
2 packages dried mushrooms
⅔ cup barley
⅓ cup finely chopped parsley

Put the meat and bones or beef base in a large pot with 4 quarts of water, the pickling spice, lemon and salt. Bring to a boil, skim the foam off and continue to skim as long as it rises to the top. Remove as much as possible. Add the mushrooms and barley, let simmer for about 2 hours. Stir occasionally to keep the barley from sticking. Remove the beef bones. Serve the meat, mushrooms and barley soup in deep plates with parsley sprinkled on top. *Serves 6 to 8.*

MENU:

ASPARAGUS VINAIGRETTE
BEEF, MUSHROOM AND BARLEY SOUP
PEAR AND CUSTARD PIE

SWEDISH STEW

A Swedish version of the Belgian carbonnade, a stew cooked with beer. The Swedish recipe also requires brandy.

2 pounds of beef rump or round steak, cut in thick slices
Flour
Salt
Freshly ground black pepper
3 tablespoons butter or bacon fat
3 tablespoons brandy
4 onions, peeled and sliced
2 cups beef bouillon
1 cup beer
6 medium potatoes, peeled and sliced
¼ cup chopped parsley

Dust the meat with the flour, salt and pepper and sauté in the fat. Add the brandy and light. When the flames die down, add the rest of the ingredients except for the potatoes and parsley. Cover and simmer over low heat for 1 hour, then add the potatoes and continue cooking until the meat and potatoes are tender. Transfer to a tureen and sprinkle with parsley. *Serves 4 to 6.*

MENU:

SWEDISH STEW
POPPYSEED ROLLS
SLICED CUCUMBERS AND RADISHES WITH SOUR CREAM DRESSING
CHERRY PIE

GULE AERTER, DANISH YELLOW SPLIT PEA SOUP

Similar to the Dutch split pea soup but different in its texture because of the boiled potatoes and salt pork. The Danes, like the French, care about the mustard they eat. Usually dry mustard is mixed with an appropriate stock, lemon juice or vinegar and sometimes horseradish.

1 pound dried yellow split peas
2 pounds salt pork or *fresh pork*
1 knob celeriac
or
1 stalk celery, with leaves, chopped
3 carrots, scraped and quartered
4 leeks, quartered
4 medium potatoes, peeled
2 small onions, peeled
½ teaspoon thyme

Soak the peas overnight in cold water, then boil them in the same water until they are soft. Remove the shells as they come to the top and discard. Drain and put through a food mill or in a blender with some of the liquid. Boil the salt pork or fresh pork in 3 quarts of water with the celery, carrots, leeks, potatoes, onions and thyme. When the vegetables are barely tender, remove and dice. When pork is tender, remove and cut into pieces and serve with sour mustard (dry mustard mixed with stock or vinegar and horseradish) on a separate plate. Skim the fat from the cooking liquid and add the pea purée and vegetables. Heat well. *Serves 4 to 6.*

MENU:

BROILED DRIED APRICOTS STUFFED WITH WATER CHESTNUTS AND WRAPPED WITH BACON
GULE AERTER
CAESAR SALAD
CORN STICKS

OXTAIL SOUP

A wonderfully sensuous soup to make as well as to eat and smell.

2 large onions, chopped
2 cloves garlic, chopped
1 stalk celery, chopped
¼ cup lard or bacon drippings
3 to 4 pounds oxtails, cut into pieces
Flour
Paprika
Salt and pepper
½ bay leaf, crumbled
1 teaspoon thyme
⅓ cup parsley, chopped
1 lemon, sliced thin
Pinch of cloves
1 tablespoon crushed peppercorns
½ teaspoon salt
3 cups beef consommé
3 cups Burgundy
1 pound green beans, cut into pieces
12 small whole white onions
1 cup diced zucchini
1 pound white grapes
Chopped fresh parsley

Sauté the onion, garlic and celery in the lard or bacon drippings. Dust the pieces of oxtails in the flour, paprika, salt and pepper. Remove the onion, garlic and celery with a slotted spoon, and put in a 2-gallon kettle. Sauté the pieces of oxtails in the same fat or drippings until brown. Add to the vegetables in the soup pot. Add the bay leaf, thyme, parsley, lemon, clove, peppercorns, salt, consommé and Burgundy. Simmer, remove the foam on the top after 20 or 30 minutes with a spoon. Continue simmering for 2 to 3 hours, adding more consommé or Burgundy if it starts to get dry. When the oxtails are fork-tender, remove from the soup pot. Strain the remaining liquid. Put back in a clean pot with the oxtails, green beans and whole onions. Simmer for about 20 or 30 minutes until the beans are almost tender but not quite. Add the zucchini and white grapes (pulled from the stems). Simmer for about 10 minutes more until the vegetables taste done but are still crisp. Put in a tureen and serve in deep soup bowls with chopped fresh parsley sprinkled over each. *Serves 4 to 6.*

MENU:

OXTAIL SOUP
BACON BISCUITS
SLICED CUCUMBERS WITH FRENCH DRESSING
STRAWBERRIES AND PINEAPPLE CHUNKS WITH THIN CUSTARD SAUCE

BORSCHT

A meat borscht is quite an undertaking—not at all like the cold dainty beet borscht served, as they say in the kosher restaurants, "with improvements."

1 quart frozen soup stock (with chunks of meat)*
¼ cup chopped celery
¼ cup chopped green pepper
2 cloves garlic, sliced thin
1 piece of bacon rind, well aged
1 (1 pound) can tomatoes
½ teaspoon freshly ground black pepper
1 tablespoon minced parsley
2 medium potatoes, diced
¼ medium cabbage, sliced thin
1 cup julienne beets (use canned and save the juice)
1 cup carrots, scraped and cut julienne
Sour cream

Put the frozen soup stock in a pot with 1 quart of water, celery, green pepper, garlic, bacon rind, tomatoes, black pepper and parsley. Bring to a boil, cook for ½ hour, add the potatoes, cook another ½ hour, add the cabbage and cook for 15 minutes more. Add the beets, juice and carrots and cook for 10 minutes more. This is better on the second or third day. Top each bowl with a spoonful of sour cream. *Serves 8 to 10.*

MENU:

HOT ANCHOVY BISCUITS
BORSCHT
FRENCH BREAD
STRAWBERRY TARTS

NAVARIN PRINTEMPS

One of the great classic stews of the French cuisine. There is a very fine line or rather a small amount of liquid that separates the soups from the stews.

- *3 pounds lamb shoulder, cut into serving pieces*
- *3 tablespoons olive oil*
- *1 tablespoon sugar*
- *Salt*
- *Freshly ground black pepper*
- *3 tablespoons flour*
- *2 to 3 cups lamb stock or canned beef bouillon*
- *2 tomatoes, peeled, seeded and chopped*
- *2 cloves garlic, finely minced*
- *¼ teaspoon thyme*
- *1 bay leaf*
- *12 small potatoes, peeled and cubed if they are too large*
- *6 carrots, scraped and cut in 1½-inch lengths*
- *6 small turnips, peeled and cubed if they are too large*
- *12 small white onions*
- *1 cup shelled peas or 1 package frozen peas*
- *1 cup green beans, cut in ½-inch lengths*

Preheat the oven to 325°. Brown the meat on all sides, a few pieces at a time, in the oil. Transfer the meat to a heavy heatproof casserole. Sprinkle the meat with the sugar and place the casserole over moderately high heat for 4 or 5 minutes. Season the meat with salt and pepper, sprinkle with flour; cook for 5 minutes longer, stirring. Add the lamb or beef stock to cover. Add the tomatoes, garlic, thyme and bay leaf and bring to a boil. Cover and bake in the oven for 1 to 1½ hours or until meat is almost tender. Remove the meat to a clean casserole. Strain the sauce, skim off the excess fat and pour the sauce over the meat. Add the potatoes, carrots, turnips and onions. Cover and bake for 25 minutes or until vegetables are almost tender. Add the peas and beans and bake for 10 minutes longer. If frozen peas are used, add them only for the last 5 minutes of baking time. *Serves 6.*

MENU:

NAVARIN PRINTEMPS
FRENCH BREAD
DANISH APPLE CRISP

WEST AFRICAN GROUND NUT STEW

With all the gay and frequent traveling to near and far places, few dishes sound really strange these days. This stew is indeed exotic but merely in the emphasis of its ingredients. Many who ate in the Tree House in the African compound at the New York World's Fair tasted this and liked it.

½ cup peanut oil
1 large onion, chopped
4 pounds stewing lamb, cubed
1 can tomato paste
2 cans beef bouillon, diluted with water
1 teaspoon chili powder
1 teaspoon anchovy paste
½ cup chunky peanut butter
1 package frozen okra

Accompaniments:
1 cup cooked crumbled bacon
2 bananas, sliced
1 cup toasted peanuts
4 hard-cooked eggs, quartered
Toasted coconut
Orange segments
½ diced red sweet pepper

In a large Dutch oven or casserole heat the peanut oil and sauté the onion and cubed lamb a little at a time over high heat, browning lightly. Mix the tomato paste with the bouillon and pour over the sautéed meat. Stir in the chili powder, anchovy paste and peanut butter. Simmer until the lamb is tender, about 1½ to 2 hours, and then add the frozen okra. Cook until the okra is tender, 10 to 15 minutes. Serve with accompaniments in small matching dishes. *Serves 6 to 8.*

MENU:

WEST AFRICAN GROUND NUT STEW
MIXED GREEN SALAD
ROTE GRUETZE

BLANQUETTE DE VEAU

The French and indeed most Europeans care more for veal than we do, and they cook it with loving care. This is a beautiful, delicate and classic dish that can only be approximated with the very best American veal. Our veal is younger than European veal, foams more when first cooked and is not exactly the same texture and color.

3 pounds veal stew meat, cut into 2-ounce, 2-inch pieces
5 to 6 cups veal stock or good chicken broth, homemade or canned
1 large onion, quartered
1 large carrot, scraped and quartered
A medium herb bouquet: 8 parsley stems (not the leaves), ½ bay leaf, ½ teaspoon thyme, 1 clove, and 2 medium celery stalks, chopped, in a cheesecloth
Salt

The Onions

18 to 24 peeled white onions, about 1 inch in diameter
½ cup of stock dipped from the simmering veal casserole
¼ teaspoon salt
1 tablespoon butter

(continued on next page)

The Sauce

4 tablespoons butter
5 tablespoons flour
3½ cups veal cooking stock
18 to 24 fresh mushroom caps about 1 inch in diameter, tossed with 1 tablespoon lemon juice
Salt and white pepper
1 to 2 tablespoons lemon juice
2 tablespoons cream or stock

The Enrichment

3 egg yolks
½ cup whipping cream
2 tablespoons minced parsley

Put the veal in an enameled pot and cover with about 2 inches of cold water. Bring to a simmer and continue for 2 minutes. Drain the veal and wash it rapidly under cold water to remove all traces of scum. Wash out the casserole. Return the meat to the casserole. Add enough stock or broth so that the veal is well covered. Bring slowly to the simmer, and skim as necessary for several minutes. Add the vegetables and herb bouquet. Taste for seasoning and salt lightly if necessary. Cover partially and simmer very slowly for 1¼ to 1½ hours, or until the veal is tender when pierced with a fork. It should not be overcooked. After peeling, cut a cross in the root ends of each onion and simmer in the half cup of stock with salt and butter for 30 to 40 minutes in a small pan, shaking now and then. When the veal is tender, pour the contents of the casserole into a colander set over a bowl. Rinse out the casserole and return the meat to the casserole, removing and discarding any loose bones. Arrange the cooked onions over the meat. Melt the butter in a saucepan, add the flour and stir over low heat until they foam together for about 2 minutes. Remove from the heat and pour in the 3½ cups of veal stock, beating vigorously with a wire whip. Bring the sauce to the boil. Simmer for 10 minutes, frequently skimming off the film which rises to the surface. Stir in the mushroom caps and simmer for 10 minutes more, skimming if still necessary. Taste the sauce very carefully for seasoning, adding salt, pepper and lemon juice to taste. Pour the sauce and mushrooms over the veal. Film the top of the sauce with 2 spoonfuls of cream or stock to prevent a skin from forming. Set aside partially covered. This much can be done ahead. About 10 to 15 minutes before serving, reheat slowly to the simmer, basting the veal with the sauce. Cover and simmer for 5 minutes. Remove from the heat. Blend the egg yolks and cream in the bowl with wire whip. Beat in by spoonfuls 1 cup of the hot sauce. Then pour the mixture into the casserole, tilting it and basting the veal and vegetables to blend the rest of the sauce with the egg-yolk mixture. Set over moderate heat, gently shaking the casserole until sauce has thickened slightly, but do not let it come to the simmer. (If not served at once, film the top of the sauce with a spoonful or two of stock, partially cover the casserole and keep warm over hot but not simmering water for 10 to 15 minutes.) Serve from the casserole or on a platter surrounded with rice, noodles or potatoes. Decorate with parsley. *Serves 6.*

MENU:

BLANQUETTE DE VEAU

NOODLES

ARTICHOKE HEARTS WITH FRENCH DRESSING

FRENCH BREAD

PEACH SHERBET

MADELINES

7

Great Soups — Chicken

There is the sound of bells, beautiful bells, in the names of some of the great soups made of chicken—waterzooie, mulligatawny, coq au vin. Some differ from stews only in the amount of liquid or the name, but who's to quibble as long as the dish is wonderful?

CHICKEN ASOPOA

In Puerto Rico a charmingly sloshy half-soup half-stew is served frequently. Preceded by a glass or two of rondo barrilito rum from the same island, asopoa is bliss indeed. Naught else is needed but some French or Italian or Cuban bread for the wonderful juices in the asopoa and some superbly fresh fruits and coffee for a graceful finale.

2 cloves garlic
1 onion, chopped
2 sweet chili peppers, seeded
1 green pepper, seeded and chopped
¼ cup lard
1 chicken (2½ to 3 pounds), cut up
2 cups rice
1 teaspoon oregano
¼ teaspoon peppercorns
3 leaves cilantro
or
1 tablespoon chopped celery leaves
or
1 teaspoon celery seed, crushed

2 teaspoons salt
Juice of ½ lime
2 tomatoes, chopped and seeded
½ cup pitted or stuffed green olives
1 tablespoon capers and 1 tablespoon caper juice
1 cup cooked peas (Puerto Ricans use canned)
1 cup chopped cooked asparagus stalks (they use canned)
1 (4-ounce) can pimentos, cut into large pieces

Sauté the garlic, onion, chili peppers and green pepper in some of the lard. When wilted but not brown, add the pieces of chicken and stir around in the mixture until they have been lightly browned. Add the rice, oregano, peppercorns, cilantro or celery leaves or celery seed, salt, lime juice, 2 cups of water, tomatoes, green olives and capers and caper juice. Simmer until tender, about 1½ hours, and add the peas, asparagus, pimentos and more liquid if needed for a somewhat liquid stew. Serve hot. *Serves 6.*

MENU:

BROILED STUFFED MUSHROOMS
CHICKEN ASOPOA
FRENCH OR ITALIAN OR CUBAN BREAD
FRESH SLICED MANGOES WITH CREAM

CHICKEN SOUP

In some cultures there is a special mystique concerning chicken soup. It is considered a panacea for all the ills that may befall a man or woman, whether emotional or physical or spiritual. This one is cheering on a dim gray day.

2 tablespoons chicken fat
2 tablespoons flour
*4 cups chicken broth**
2 cups heavy cream
2 egg yolks
1 cup cooked chicken breast, cut julienne
⅓ cup parsley

Melt the chicken fat, blend in the flour and cook for about 5 minutes. Add the broth a little at a time, stirring constantly with a wire whisk until thin and smooth. Add 1 cup of cream, beat the other cup or put in a blender with the egg yolks. Stir in the soup and cook until smooth and thickened. Add the chicken meat, which has been cut julienne, and parsley. *Serves 6.*

Basic chicken broth

1 chicken (about 4½ pounds), cut into pieces
1 large leek, sliced
½ cup diced white turnips
2 large white onions, quartered
1 small bunch green onions
1 bay leaf
¼ teaspoon thyme
⅛ teaspoon cloves
⅛ teaspoon powdered mace
Salt
1 teaspoon crushed peppercorns

Put the chicken pieces into a pot with 3 quarts of cold water, cover and bring to a boil. Skim off the foam, and continue skimming it off until as much as possible has been removed. This is necessary for a lovely clear broth. To the chicken and water add the leek, turnip, onion, green onions, bay leaf, thyme, cloves, mace, salt and peppercorns. Cover and simmer for 2½ to 3 hours. Remove the chicken from the broth and strain. Pour into a bowl and chill thoroughly. Remove the seasoned fat and save. Use in the cream soup or in other cooking. Refrigerate the broth or pour into an ice-cube tray and freeze in cubes. Later package the cubes in Pliofilm bags. Measure the capacity of an ice cube in your tray—sizes vary—by melting one in a measuring cup, and use accordingly. Remove the chicken meat from the bones and refrigerate or freeze for soup or other dishes.

MENU:

CHICKEN SOUP
POPOVERS
BROILED SALMON STEAKS
FRESH PEAS
WATERCRESS WITH ROQUEFORT DRESSING
BLACKBERRY FLUMMERY

COCK-A-LEEKIE SOUP

The name of this Scotch classic is more familiar than the soup itself with its unusual flavors. There are places and times when airily calling for 2 bunches of leeks may sound as if one were very rich and reckless—when 1 leek is selling for 15 to 20 cents. Green onions can be used, but the texture and the flavor are different—and the name becomes inaccurate.

2 large bunches leeks
or
2 large bunches green onions

1 aged fowl (about 5 pounds)
2 cups beef bouillon
1 box tenderized prunes
Salt and pepper

Cut and discard the green part of the leeks. Cut the white part in 1-inch lengths and cut in half lengthwise. Wash carefully to remove the sand. Simmer the leeks and fowl in the beef bouillon for 2½ to 3 hours until the chicken is tender. Remove the grease from the top of the liquid by blotting it with a paper towel, or strain, chill and remove the grease. Cut the chicken into serving-size pieces and reheat with the strained broth. Add the prunes, salt and pepper and heat until the prunes are tender. Serve in a tureen. *Serves 6 to 8.*

MENU:

HOT SMOKY PEA PUFFS
COCK-A-LEEKIE SOUP
TOASTED ENGLISH MUFFINS
SALAD OF TOMATO QUARTERS, DICED AVOCADO, HARD-COOKED EGGS QUARTERED AND FRENCH DRESSING
GINGERBREAD WITH WHIPPED CREAM

MULLIGATAWNY SOUP

There are many versions of this East Indian chicken soup seasoned with curry.

2 tablespoons butter
¼ pound diced salt pork
1 chicken (2½ pounds), cut up
1 tablespoon flour
1 to 2 heaping teaspoons Madras curry powder
2 quarts chicken or veal stock
½ cup diced carrots
1 stalk celery, chopped
2 onions, chopped
1 apple, peeled, cored and chopped
1 bay leaf
2 whole cloves
6 peppercorns, slightly cracked
½ cup light cream
Rice
Parsley

Melt the butter in a skillet, add the diced salt pork and brown slightly. Add pieces of chicken and sauté over low heat until light-colored. Strew the flour and curry powder over the chicken and allow this to cook with it briefly. Transfer to a soup kettle, juices and all. Add the chicken or veal stock, carrot, celery, onion, apple, bay leaf, cloves and peppercorns. Bring to a boil and then turn the heat down very low to a simmer. Skim off the surface, add 1 cup of cold water, bring to a boil again, skim again; then turn heat down and simmer until the chicken is tender, about 1 hour or longer. Remove the chicken from the stock and cut the meat from the bones into neat pieces. Put the meat aside if the soup is not to be served at this moment. Strain the broth and remove any fat from it. This can be done more easily if there is time to chill the broth first thoroughly. To serve, heat the chicken in the broth and check the seasonings. Add the cream. This is served with a bowl of plain boiled rice, dry and flaky. A spoonful of rice is put in each soup plate and then sprinkled with finely chopped parsley. Spoon the soup and meat over it. *Serves 4 to 6.*

MENU:

HOT CLAM AND SPINACH SHELLS
MULLIGATAWNY SOUP
FRENCH BREAD
PEAR SHERBET WITH RASPBERRIES

WATERZOOIE

This might be called the national dish of Belgium. It is delicate and rich and satisfying, as most Belgian cooking is. Even the French often concede the superiority of the Belgians in some areas of cooking.

¼ cup butter
1 capon (7 to 8 pounds), cut into large pieces
4 leeks, washed and trimmed
8 ribs celery, coarsely chopped
1 carrot, scraped and coarsely chopped
1 small onion, quartered
4 sprigs parsley
¼ teaspoon thyme
¼ teaspoon nutmeg
½ bay leaf
4 cloves
6 cups chicken broth
1 lemon, thinly sliced
1 tablespoon chopped parsley
4 egg yolks
¼ cup heavy cream

Heat the butter in a skillet and brown the capon on all sides. Place the capon with the vegetables and seasonings in a heatproof casserole. Cover with chicken broth and bring to a boil. Reduce the heat and simmer until tender, 2 to 3 hours. Remove the capon from the liquid. Remove and discard the skin and bones. Cut the meat into large pieces and save. Strain the liquid and skim off the excess fat. Place over high heat and reduce liquid. Add the lemon and chopped parsley. Turn heat down. Beat the egg yolks and cream together. Stir into the soup and allow to thicken slightly, but do not boil. Add the pieces of chicken and heat briefly. *Serves 6 to 8.*

MENU:

WATERZOOIE
FRENCH BREAD
BELGIAN ENDIVE SALAD
CHARLOTTE MALAKOFF

COQ AU VIN

One of the classic French dishes which disproves the cliché of white wine always with fowl and red always with meat. This uses either white or red, but the red is more usual. In the classic version of this dish, the liquid is reduced by simmering for about 2½ hours. But that is much too long for our tender young chickens. This version is adapted to the brief cooking they need.

3 slices lean bacon, cut into inch pieces
1 chicken (2½ pounds), cut into serving pieces
½ teaspoon salt
⅛ teaspoon pepper
12 small white onions
2 cloves garlic, finely minced
¼ cup cognac
2 cups full-bodied red wine (such as Burgundy or Beaujolais)
1 cup canned beef gravy
1 teaspoon tomato paste
¼ teaspoon thyme
1 bay leaf
½ pound mushroom caps, sautéed in butter until tender

In a heavy, heatproof casserole, cook the bacon gently, pouring off the drippings as it cooks—leaving about 2 tablespoons. Pour out some of the fat. Sprinkle the chicken with the salt and pepper and add to the casserole. Cook until well browned on all sides. Add the onions and garlic and cook gently for about 2 minutes. Add the cognac and ignite. When flames die down, add the wine. Mix the beef gravy with the tomato paste and add. Add the thyme and bay leaf, cover and simmer gently until the chicken is done, 25 minutes longer. Before serving, add the mushrooms and adjust the seasonings. If sauce is too thin, thicken with a little cornstarch mixed to a paste with more of the red wine. *Serves 4.*

MENU:

COQ AU VIN
FRENCH BREAD
PARSLEY POTATOES
CHOCOLATE CAKE

CHICKEN PAPRIKA WITH SPAETZLE

It is not true that all meat dishes in Hungary are cooked with paprika and sour cream, but some of their finest dishes are. The Hungarian prefers the sweet rose paprika that in this country is bought at specialty food stores like Paprikas Weiss at 1504 Second Avenue, New York City. Like other specialists in Middle European foods, this shop carries paprika in two other strengths, the medium hot and the hot hot. They are not for the unwary. No Hungarian will seriously consider the red dust labeled as paprika in most supermarkets.

2 large onions, chopped
1 clove garlic, chopped fine
3 tablespoons butter
2 broiler-size chickens (2½ pounds each), cut up
1 tablespoon Hungarian rose paprika
1 cup chicken stock
2 teaspoons salt
1 cup sour cream
Spaetzle

Sauté the onion and garlic in butter. Add the chicken. Sprinkle with the paprika. Brown the chicken. Add the chicken stock, salt and cover. Simmer for 25 minutes. Add the sour cream, cook the sauce for 5 minutes more being careful not to let boil. Serve in a tureen with spaetzle or soft noodles on the side. *Serves 4 to 6.*

Spaetzle

Beat 2 eggs and add 1½ cups of flour and a pinch of salt. Add about ½ cup of water, a little at a time. The dough should be soft but not too runny. The size of eggs varies slightly, as does the moisture in the flour and indeed the flour itself. Let the dough stand for about 30 minutes. Either drop in boiling salted water by the teaspoon or push through the holes of a colander or pat on a wet breadboard and cut off small pieces with a wet knife. When the spaetzle come to the top of the water, they are done.

MENU:

CHICKEN PAPRIKA WITH SPAETZLE
SLICED AVOCADO AND WATERCRESS SALAD
COLD LEMON SOUFFLÉ

BRUNSWICK STEW

Originally Brunswick stew used rabbit or squirrel more often than chicken; now chicken is the usual version along with tomatoes, corn, lima beans and onions, and sometimes okra. In Virginia it is often cooked briefly enough so that the vegetables are still distinguishable. Farther south, they are apt to be almost cooked to a purée.

2 chickens (about 2½ pounds each), cut up
1 tablespoon salt
2 cups chopped onions
1 large can tomatoes
1 pound fresh shelled lima beans or 2 packages frozen
1 box fresh okra or 1 package frozen
2 cups whole kernel corn, fresh, frozen or canned
½ teaspoon Tabasco sauce

Put the chicken in a large pot of water with the salt and cook slowly until tender, 45 minutes to 1 hour. Remove from the liquid and save the broth for some other meal. Remove the meat from the bones and cut into pieces. Put chicken in a pot with all the vegetables except the corn and 2 cups of the broth. Cook slowly until the limas are tender, add the corn and Tabasco sauce in the last 15 minutes. *Serves 4 to 6.*

MENU:

HUSH PUPPIES
BRUNSWICK STEW
LEAF LETTUCE WITH HOT BACON DRESSING
PINEAPPLE SHERBET WITH FRESH STRAWBERRIES

8

Classic and Sustaining with Meat

People all around the world have been nourished day in and day out by soups like these. They are a robust mélange of the good things at hand. These, in this chapter, are derived from affluent times and countries and contain generous amounts of meat.

CHICKEN AND LEMON SOUP

All Mediterranean soups have some relation to one another, no matter what the country. This one obviously was first concocted by someone familiar with the Greek avgolemono soup or perhaps inspired by the same ingredients.

4 cups chicken broth
2 teaspoons grated lemon peel
Juice of ½ lemon
¼ cup sherry or white wine
2 cooked chicken breasts
1 tablespoon cornstarch
2 egg yolks, lightly beaten
½ cup pineapple chunks
4 sprigs watercress
Slivered almonds

Simmer the broth with the lemon peel, lemon juice and wine for about 30 minutes, so that the wine does not taste "raw." Add the chicken breasts, skinned, boned and cut in strips, to the broth and wine. Mix the cornstarch with a little water to make a paste and add to the broth, stirring until slightly thickened. Beat a little of the liquid into the eggs and then add to the other liquids, stirring over low heat for just a few minutes. Serve the soup with some of the chicken strips and pineapple chunks in each bowl. Put a sprig of the watercress in each and sprinkle with slivered almonds.
Serves 4.

MENU:

CHICKEN AND LEMON SOUP
CHEESE SOUFFLÉ
BELGIAN ENDIVE
PEACH SHERBET

SWEDISH BEEF AND PEA SOUP

Unlike most soups made with dried legumes, this one has a large amount of meat. It is indeed what might be called a Swedish version of pot-au-feu.

2½ pounds lean beef brisket, in 1 piece
1 teaspoon pepper
1½ teaspoons salt
½ pound dried whole green peas, soaked overnight if not ready-to-cook
1 small green cabbage, cut in eighths
3 medium potatoes, peeled and quartered
6 tiny carrots, scraped and cut in half lengthwise

Put the brisket in a soup pot with the pepper and salt. Add water to cover. Simmer for 2½ to 3 hours. Drain the peas and add them to the liquid with the cabbage, potatoes and carrots. Cook for 1 hour longer. Skim off any fat that rises to the surface and check the seasoning. The easiest way to remove the fat is to chill it first, but this takes time. To serve, cut the meat in thin slices and put in a tureen with the vegetables and broth. *Serves 6 to 8.*

MENU:

SWEDISH BEEF AND PEA SOUP
FRENCH BREAD
SLICED CUCUMBER AND WATERCRESS SALAD
GRAPEFRUIT SECTIONS WITH DICED PRESERVED KUMQUAT

GIBLET SOUP

Not only simple to make, good to eat, but this is also a reasonably inexpensive soup. It can be made with the giblets from 4 chickens or in somewhat larger amounts with the giblets, hearts, gizzards and liver bought separately. If made from giblets of chickens you have, use the necks, but it isn't important to buy them. There are some who call this mock turtle soup, but it is doubtful whether they have ever tasted real turtle soup.

1 medium onion, chopped
1 piece celery, chopped
½ green pepper, chopped
2 tablespoons butter
½ pound chicken hearts, cut into small pieces
½ pound chicken gizzards, cut into small pieces
1 tablespoon flour
2 quarts chicken broth and water or all water
¼ pound chicken livers
1 tablespoon butter
1 tablespoon flour
Salt and pepper
3 hard-cooked eggs

Sauté the onion and celery and green pepper in the butter until somewhat wilted-looking. Add the chicken hearts and gizzards. Sprinkle with the flour. Cook for a few minutes and then put in a pot with the chicken broth and/or water. Simmer for about 1½ hours or until tender. Sauté the chicken livers in the butter. Add the flour. The original directions say to rub the livers through a fine sieve and add them to the soup kettle with 1 tablespoon of butter and 1 tablespoon of flour, which have been browned together. But, it is simpler if one has a blender to purée the livers with a ladle of the broth and then add to the soup. Bring to a boil again and cook for a few minutes. Season to taste with salt and pepper. Just before serving, stir in the hard-cooked eggs, which have been coarsely chopped. *Serves 6.*

MENU:

FRESH BUTTERED TOAST
AVOCADO, GRAPEFRUIT AND WATERCRESS SALAD
MACAROON SOUFFLÉ

SOUP WITH ALBONDIGAS

In New Mexico, in days not too long past, food was often very scarce and a little bit was made to go a long way. Meatballs or albondigas were made from all sorts of meat scraps ground together. These meatballs with a Mexican flavor were served in a hot thick chili sauce or in broth and sometimes just in water that got its flavor from the meatballs. This recipe obviously has been adapted to our affluent society.

1 pound ground beef
1 pound ground pork
1 cup soft bread crumbs
or
⅓ cup cornmeal
1 egg, slightly beaten
1 clove garlic, chopped
½ teaspoon oregano
½ teaspoon cumin
4 cups beef bouillon
2 teaspoons dried mint leaves
½ teaspoon saffron

Mix the beef, pork, bread crumbs or cornmeal, egg, garlic, oregano and cumin together. Form into small balls about the size of cherry tomatoes. Simmer the meatballs or albondigas in the beef broth with the mint leaves and saffron for 30 to 45 minutes. *Serves 6 amply.*

MENU:

SOUP WITH ALBONDIGAS
CORN TOAST
ENCHILADAS

ONE MEATBALL SOUP

In the Near East, the one meatball, a large one, is served in soup in a tureen and carved with a splendid gesture by the host. One slice is placed in each bowl and the soup ladled over it.

1 lamb bone with a little meat on it
1 onion, sliced
1 clove garlic
1 carrot, sliced
Salt and pepper
¼ teaspoon rosemary
2 egg yolks
Juice of 1 lemon

Meatball

1 pound lamb shoulder, ground
1 cup cooked rice
⅓ cup finely chopped fresh parsley
Salt and pepper
1 egg, slightly beaten

Stuffing

1 large or 2 small Bermuda onions, chopped
3 tablespoons butter
3 tablespoons currants
3 tablespoons pine nuts or pignolias
½ teaspoon allspice
½ teaspoon cinnamon

For the soup, simmer the lamb bone, onion, garlic, carrot, salt, pepper and rosemary in 2 quarts of water for 2 hours; skim off the fat and strain the broth. Bring to a boil.

Mix the ground lamb with the cooked rice, parsley, salt, pepper and egg. Pat into a large ball, smooth and round. For the stuffing, sauté the chopped onion in the butter, remove from the fire and add the currants, pine nuts and seasonings. Stir around briefly to mix. Chill for easier handling. Punch a hole in the meatball, poke the filling in and pat the hole closed. Tie the ball in a piece of cheesecloth—or a man's sheer handkerchief—so that all will stay together, and drop into the boiling broth. Cook until the meatball is done, about 40 to 50 minutes. Remove the ball from the pan, take off the cheesecloth and put the meat in a warm place. Beat the egg yolks with the lemon juice and add to the soup. Stir until smooth and thickened. Serve in a warm tureen for a flourish or in individual soup bowls. Carve the meatball with a grand gesture at the table and serve each person one slice in his bowl of soup. *Serves 4 generously.*

MENU:

ONE MEATBALL SOUP
ARMENIAN BREAD
SLICED CUCUMBERS
APRICOT SPONGE

CHICKEN AND SPINACH SOUP

Green and delicate and lovely.

4 chicken breasts, boned and skinned
1 pound spinach, washed and stemmed
or
1 package frozen chopped spinach
2 tablespoons butter
2 tablespoons flour
3 cups chicken broth
½ cup sour cream
Salt and pepper

Simmer the chicken breasts in about a cup of water until tender and use this liquid as part of the cooking liquid. Steam the spinach in the water that clings to the leaves after washing, for about 6 minutes or until soft—less time for the frozen spinach. Melt the butter in a saucepan, add the flour and cook for a few minutes. Add 1 cup of chicken broth, a little at a time, stirring constantly until smooth and thickened. Add the drained cooked spinach (the fresh must be chopped), the rest of the chicken broth and the chicken breasts. When very hot, remove from the stove and add the sour cream. Check the seasoning and add more if it needs it. Some chicken broths have more than others. Serve with a chicken breast in each soup bowl. The chicken breasts can be cut in bite-sized pieces if you do not want to serve knives and forks for cutting, but a whole breast in each bowl is more dramatic. *Serves 4.*

MENU:

CHICKEN AND SPINACH SOUP
CHEESE TRIANGLES
DRIED FRUITS AND NUTS

BULGARIAN LAMB SOUP

Similar ingredients to those of lamb stews elsewhere but with a subtly different emphasis—no carrots, and an egg and lemon and yoghurt thickening that is pleasing and unexpected.

½ pound shoulder lamb, fat removed and diced
1 teaspoon salt
3 tomatoes, peeled, seeded and chopped
3 green peppers, seeded and chopped
1 large onion, chopped
2 tablespoons rice
2 tablespoons butter
2 tablespoons flour
1 cup lamb broth
2 egg yolks, slightly beaten
½ cup yoghurt
Grated peel and juice of ½ lemon
Salt and pepper
Finely chopped parsley

Sprinkle the lamb with the teaspoon of salt. Put in a pan with 6 cups of cold water. Bring to a boil, then turn down to a simmer. Cook the meat for about 20 minutes until nearly tender. Add the tomatoes, green peppers, onion and rice. Cook for about 15 minutes longer. In a small saucepan melt the butter and blend in the flour. Slowly add 1 cup of strained lamb broth from the pot. Cook the sauce, stirring constantly until it is thick and smooth. Gradually stir into the soup and cook for about 5 minutes. Then stir the egg yolks into the yoghurt. Add the juice and grated lemon peel. Turn the heat down, so that the soup does not boil. Then add the yoghurt mixture, salt and pepper to taste. When serving, sprinkle the soup with the finely chopped parsley. *Serves 5 or 6.*

MENU:

BULGARIAN LAMB SOUP
RYE BREAD
CUCUMBER AND RED ONION SALAD
SLICED FRESH ORANGES WITH CURAÇAO

A ROBUST SOUP, ALMOST A STEW

A good Sunday night supper dish that waits amiably.

2 pounds beef round, cut into chunks
2 cups Burgundy
2 cups bouillon, canned or cubes, diluted
1 lemon, sliced thin
1 fat clove garlic, cut in half
1 bay leaf
Olive oil
8 small or 4 large onions, quartered
3 medium potatoes, peeled and quartered
1 can Italian tomato paste
Salt and peppercorns
1 can water chestnuts, sliced (nice not obligatory)

Marinate the meat overnight in the wine, bouillon, with the lemon, garlic and bay leaf. Remove the meat from the marinade, dry and sauté in the oil. Add the cooked meat to the strained marinade along with the onions, potatoes and tomato paste. Simmer gently for about 2 hours. Season and serve or keep and reheat later. Add sliced water chestnuts. *Serves 6 to 8.*

MENU:

A ROBUST SOUP, ALMOST A STEW
FRENCH BREAD
GRAPEFRUIT SEGMENTS, FINELY CHOPPED GREEN ONION, PIMENTO AND FRENCH DRESSING

POTAGE SAINT-HUBERT

There are quite a few European soups with this name. Saint Hubert is the patron saint of hunters, so that constant to soups of this name is wild game. Some of the best are made with pheasant, but others are made with wild duck, rabbit or wild goose. It would be extravagant to buy a pheasant or other game for this soup, but if you have a hunter in the family or generous hunter friends, then use it this way. The soup can be frozen and kept for another day.

1 roasted pheasant, duck, goose or rabbit	*½ teaspoon thyme*
2 cups lentils, soaked	*½ bay leaf*
	Salt and pepper
1 onion, quartered	*½ cup heavy cream*

Pull the meat from the bones. Dice the neatest pieces and save for later. Put the raggedy pieces and the bones in a pan with the lentils, onion, thyme, bay leaf and pepper. Add salted water (the exact amount does not matter too much) and simmer until the lentils are tender, which will vary according to their unknown age. Remove from the fire, fish out the bones and discard. Purée the meat and lentils in a food mill or a blender. Return to the heat, add enough of the lentil liquor until the soup is the right consistency (thick). Check the seasonings and add more, if necessary. When hot, add the cream and diced pheasant. *Serves 8.*

MENU:

POTAGE SAINT-HUBERT

FRENCH BREAD

WATERCRESS AND GRAPEFRUIT SALAD WITH FRENCH DRESSING AND SPRINKLED WITH POMEGRANATE SEEDS

SWEDISH CHICKEN SOUP WITH CHICKEN QUENELLES

A very elegant but simple to prepare chicken soup with chicken quenelles. In Norway it is called the Queen soup. The chicken quenelles must be made a little ahead of time so that they can be chilled enough to mold.

Soup

4 egg yolks
⅓ cup light cream
¼ cup sherry
6½ cups boiling hot chicken broth, homemade or canned
Chicken quenelles

Put the egg yolks, cream and sherry in a blender and blend briefly. Pour into a warm soup tureen and add the seasoned hot chicken broth slowly, beating with a whisk. Add the chicken quenelles and serve. *Serves 6 to 8.*

Chicken quenelles

2 cups diced raw chicken breast
6 tablespoons melted butter
2 eggs
1 tablespoon heavy cream or sour cream
1 teaspoon salt

Put the diced chicken meat in a blender (or several times through a meat grinder with the finest blade) with the melted butter, eggs, cream and salt. Blend until velvety smooth. Chill until firm enough to make into small oval balls that will hold their shape. Use a teaspoon to shape them. Drop them into rapidly boiling salted water. Cook for 8 to 10 minutes. Remove with a slotted spoon. Add to the soup in the tureen and serve. *Enough for 6 soup bowls or more.*

MENU:

SWEDISH CHICKEN SOUP WITH CHICKEN QUENELLES
ROAST FILLET OF BEEF
BROILED MUSHROOM CAPS
BAKED POTATOES
DRIED FRUIT COMPOTE (dried apricots, peaches and pears, soaked in white wine for several days and sprinkled with grated orange peel and pine nuts)

STUFFED PEPPER SOUP

Somewhere between a soup and a stew and certainly a meal in itself except for the very hearty.

½ pound chopped beef
¼ pound chopped pork
¼ pound chopped veal
1 medium onion, chopped
⅓ cup cooked rice
Salt and pepper
4 medium green peppers
3 cans condensed tomato soup, undiluted
2 cloves garlic, cut in half
Sour cream

Mix the chopped meats, onion, rice and seasoning together. Cut the tops off the peppers and rinse out the seeds with water. Fill with the meat mixture. Put the stuffed peppers in a pot or a deep baking dish with the tomato soup and cut cloves of garlic. Cook over low heat or in a 350° oven, tightly covered, 45 minutes to 1 hour. Fish out the garlic before serving. Serve a pepper and some sauce in each soup bowl with a spoonful of sour cream on top. *Serves 4.*

MENU:

STUFFED PEPPER SOUP
WATERCRESS AND ROMAINE SALAD WITH GRAPEFRUIT SEGMENTS AND FRENCH DRESSING
HOT CORN BREAD
FRESH STRAWBERRY TARTS

PEASANT SOUP
(For a large group)

A beautiful and aromatic and exciting soup to serve at an informal party. It is simple to make, can be made ahead of time and frozen (except for the macaroni shells) until needed.

2 veal shanks (2 pounds meat each)
4 teaspoons salt
½ teaspoon pepper
¼ cup cooking oil
½ cup chopped celery
½ cup chopped fresh spinach
½ cup chopped green pepper
½ cup chopped onion
½ pound pepperoni, sliced thin
2 cups peeled and diced potatoes
2 cups peeled and diced turnips
2 cups scraped and diced carrots
2 cups uncooked small macaroni shells
1 (1-pound, 14-ounce) can tomatoes
1 (10-ounce) package frozen peas
3¾ cups canned beef broth
1 clove garlic, minced
¼ teaspoon dried basil
Grated Parmesan cheese

Put the veal shanks in a deep kettle; add 3 quarts of water, 2 teaspoons of the salt and ¼ teaspoon of the pepper. Cover and heat until boiling. Reduce the heat and simmer for about 2 hours or until the meat is fork-tender. Allow the meat to cool in the broth. Remove the bones and meat. Cut the meat off the bones into bite-size pieces. Chill the broth. Remove the fat from the surface. Heat the cooking oil in a skillet and sauté the celery, spinach, green pepper and onion until the onion is golden. Heat the veal broth until simmering and add the contents of the skillet and the pepperoni, potatoes, turnips and carrots. Simmer until the vegetables are almost tender. Cook the macaroni shells according to the package directions. Drain well and add to the soup. Add the veal, tomatoes, peas and beef broth. Season with the remaining salt and pepper, garlic and basil and serve. This much can be done ahead of time. If desired, cool, pack into containers, cover and freeze, omitting the macaroni. To serve, allow soup to thaw at room temperature. Cook the macaroni shells and add to the soup. Reheat slowly until very hot. Serve sprinkled with Parmesan cheese. *Makes 6 to 7 quarts. Serves 15 to 20.*

MENU:

PEASANT SOUP FRENCH BREAD
MIXED GREEN SALAD MELON

LAMB STEW WITH OKRA

This is one of the most beautiful of all stews, simple to make and not fattening, whether counting calories or carbohydrates.

1 pound lamb or beef, cubed
4 tablespoons butter
2 large onions, diced
or
12 small white onions
1 (1-pound, 14-ounce) can tomatoes
1 pound fresh okra, with the tops removed
or
1 package frozen okra, thawed
½ teaspoon thyme
Salt and pepper
1 lemon, sliced thin

Sauté the meat lightly in the butter, add the onions and cook over medium heat for 5 minutes for the diced onions, 10 to 15 minutes for the whole ones. Add the tomatoes, okra, seasoning and lemon. Cover and cook over medium heat until the meat is tender, which will vary, of course, according to the quality of the meat. Add water if it starts to dry out. It should have a rather sloshy consistency. *Serves 4.*

MENU:

LAMB STEW WITH OKRA
CHOPPED CUCUMBER WITH YOGHURT AND FRESH MINT
FRESH BING CHERRIES

KIDNEY SOUP

Those without a spirit of gastronomic adventure who abjure all variety meats miss some culinary bliss. The kidneys, hearts and livers have excitingly varied textures, flavor and nutrition. Often they are inexpensive. Some make delectable soups.

2 onions, finely chopped
½ stick butter
12 lamb kidneys, quartered
or
2 veal kidneys, cut apart
1 tablespoon Hungarian sweet rose paprika
1 tablespoon flour
1 pint beef bouillon
1 teaspoon grated lemon peel
1 cup heavy cream
¼ cup French dry vermouth
Salt and pepper
2 tablespoons lemon juice
2 tablespoons sweet butter

Sauté the onions in the ½ stick of butter until soft and wilted but not brown. Add the kidneys, from which all specks of white have been cut and discarded. Stir them into the onion-and-butter mixture over low heat for 3 or 4 minutes. Sprinkle with the paprika and flour and stir some more. Add the beef bouillon and lemon peel. Simmer for about ½ hour or more and then add the heavy cream and vermouth, salt and pepper. Heat thoroughly. Just before serving, finish with the lemon juice and the sweet butter stirred in quickly. *Serves 4 to 6.*

MENU:

KIDNEY SOUP
POPPYSEED ROLLS
FRESH FRUITS WITH SOUR CREAM AND DICED CRYSTALLIZED GINGER

MENUDA

This is a tripe soup much loved by Spaniards and Mexicans for such festive occasions as Christmas Eve and New Year's. It is also good for a late, leisurely breakfast.

3 pounds honeycomb tripe, cut into 1-inch squares
Veal knuckle, cracked
4 cloves garlic, cut in halves
2 large onions, chopped
1 teaspoon coriander
2 teaspoons oregano
2 tablespoons chili powder
1 (20-ounce) can whole hominy
Chopped green onions
Chopped canned green chilies
Fresh cilantro or Chinese parsley or mint

Cook the tripe, veal knuckle, garlic, onion and seasonings in 2 quarts of water in a deep pot for 4 to 6 hours or until the tripe is tender. Remove the veal knuckle, add the hominy and reheat. This much can be done ahead. Correct the seasonings. Serve in large shallow soup plates. Pass separate bowls of chopped green onions, chopped green chilies and fresh cilantro or Chinese parsley or fresh mint and let each person sprinkle some of these over his soup plate. *Serves 6 to 8.*

MENU:

ORANGE SECTIONS, PINEAPPLE CHUNKS AND BING CHERRIES WITH COINTREAU
MENUDA
BRIOCHES
GINGER MARMALADE

CHICKEN AND CORN SOUP

Most people think of this as typically American. I pinpoint it much more regionally and think of it as Pennsylvanian and Pennsylvania Dutch.

1 chicken (5 pounds), cut into serving pieces
Salt
12 peppercorns
2 ribs celery, chopped
2 carrots, scraped and quartered
1 whole onion
6 ears of corn on the cob
or
2 cups frozen corn
2 hard-cooked eggs, sliced
1 tablespoon finely chopped parsley
1 cup cubed ham

Put the chicken in a deep kettle with water to cover, salt, peppercorns, celery, carrots and onion. Simmer until the chicken is thoroughly tender. Remove the chicken from the broth, strain the broth and pour into a clean deep pan. Simmer to reduce a little more. Pull the chicken from the bones, discard the skin and bones. Cut the chicken into bite-size pieces. Husk the corn and put it into the broth and bring to a boil. Remove and cut the kernels from the cobs into the soup. The Pennsylvania Dutch never never use anything but the most impeccably fresh ingredients. It *is* possible to use 2 or 3 packages of frozen cut corn. Add the chicken, the hard-cooked eggs, parsley and ham and heat thoroughly. Serve piping hot. *Serves 8 to 12.*

MENU:

CHICKEN AND CORN SOUP
HOT BISCUITS
WATERCRESS AND ENDIVE SALAD WITH VINAIGRETTE DRESSING
STRAWBERRY SOUFFLÉ

PORK GOULASH

Those who have not tasted veal or pork cooked with sauerkraut and sour cream do not know quite how heavenly the flavor can be. Unless of German extraction, Americans tend to have sauerkraut with hot dogs, period, and seldom adventure further into the truly delectable dishes based on it like this one.

1 pork loin (4 to 5 pounds), boned and cubed
3 tablespoons lard
4 large onions, sliced
2 tablespoons paprika
1 teaspoon salt
½ teaspoon marjoram
2 cloves garlic, minced
1 cup pork broth or chicken broth
1 (1-pound, 13-ounce) can sauerkraut, rinsed and squeezed dry
1 cup sour cream
¼ cup kümmel or Tokay wine (optional)

Brown the pork in the lard, remove, brown the onions in the same fat until golden. Add the pork and sprinkle with paprika and salt. Add the marjoram, garlic and broth. Simmer, covered, for about 30 minutes. Add the sauerkraut and cook until the pork is tender, about 30 minutes more. Stir in the sour cream, kümmel or Tokay and heat, do not boil.

To make pork broth, simmer 1 pound of cracked pork bones and 2 cups of water with a little salt for 1 hour, and strain. *Serves 8.*

MENU:

PORK GOULASH
NOODLES
WALDORF SALAD
POPPY SEED ROLLS
CHERRY STRUDEL

VEAL GOULASH

Rather simple and rather wonderful.

2 pounds boneless leg of veal, cut into 1½-inch cubes
2 teaspoons salt
2 teaspoons Hungarian sweet rose paprika
¼ cup (½ stick) butter
2 cups sliced onion
3 large tomatoes, peeled and diced
1 cup sour cream
2 teaspoons caraway seeds
Juice of one lemon
Chicken broth
*Spaetzle**

Sprinkle the veal with the salt and paprika, and brown the meat on all sides in very hot butter. Add the onion and tomatoes, stirring until most of the liquid is gone. Add the sour cream, caraway seeds and lemon juice. Cover and cook over very low heat until the veal is tender, about 1 hour. Check at intervals and add a little chicken broth if necessary for a saucelike consistency. Serve the veal and sauce with spaetzle (cooked noodles). *Serves 6.*

MENU:

VEAL GOULASH
NOODLES OR SPAETZLE
TOMATO ASPIC WITH HEARTS OF ARTICHOKE
APPLE FRITTERS WITH POWDERED SUGAR

PICADILLO WITH RICE AND BEANS

A fine Spanish or Mexican mishmash of meat and raisins, and sometimes olives or nuts, which is usually served with rice and beans. The beans can be garbanzos or chick-peas, pink Mexican beans or red kidney beans or, handsomest of all, black beans. Usually the black beans must be bought dried and soaked and simmered with a ham hock until tender, but increasingly the black beans can be found canned in sections of the country where South Americans live.

1 medium onion, minced
1 clove garlic, minced
4 tablespoons olive oil
1½ pounds chopped beef
2 cups canned tomatoes
2 tablespoons raisins
1 teaspoon dry hot chili pepper
1 teaspoon vinegar
Salt and pepper
4 cups cooked rice
3 cups cooked black or other beans
1 hard-cooked egg white, chopped
½ cup slivered almonds

Sauté the onion and garlic in the olive oil. Add the beef, tomatoes, raisins, chili pepper, vinegar, salt and pepper. Simmer for about 30 minutes. While this is called a stew, it is served rather dry with fluffy white rice and black beans or other beans. Sprinkle the top with chopped hard-cooked egg white and almonds. *Serves 4 to 6.*

MENU:

PICADILLO WITH RICE AND BEANS
WATERCRESS AND GRAPEFRUIT SALAD WITH FRENCH DRESSING
HOT ROLLS
FLAN

9

Classic and Sustaining with Little Meat

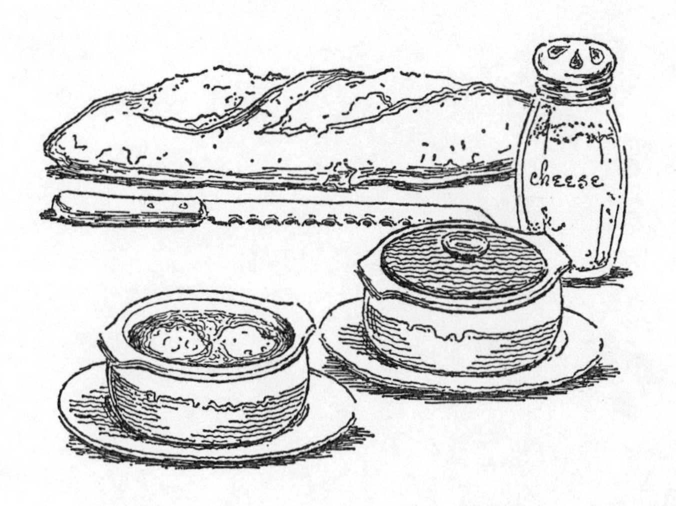

Imaginative cooks all through the ages have been able to make delectable soups with small amounts of meat and lots of vegetables, dumplings and other robust fillers.

PENNSYLVANIA DUTCH SOUP WITH DOUGH BALLS

This fascinating and spicy soup with small sausage balls and small dough balls bobbing around in it was traditionally made with a calf's head. Like so many others of my somewhat sheltered generation, I would rather cook the veal shin than look my meat in the eye, as it were. Besides, it isn't easy to find calves' heads these days except in some sections in large cities catering to the foreign-born.

1 veal shin with meat
3 medium potatoes, peeled and diced
1 medium onion, diced
2 tablespoons butter
½ pound fresh sausage meat
½ teaspoon marjoram
¼ teaspoon cloves
¼ teaspoon allspice
2 hard-cooked eggs, diced
½ cup flour

Cook the veal shin in 2 quarts of salted water for several hours until quite tender. Cook the potatoes and onion in the butter for about 20 minutes over low heat. Make the sausage into 1-inch balls and fry until brown. Make the dough balls as in the following recipe. When the meat is tender remove from the broth, cool slightly and pull from the bones and cube. Put back in the broth with the potatoes, onion, sausage balls, spices, diced eggs and dough balls. Stir in the flour, which has been browned and stirred in the dry pan over medium heat and then mixed to a smooth paste with 1 cup of the broth. Simmer all together for 5 minutes. *Serves 8 in the generous Pennsylvania Dutch fashion.*

The Dough Balls

1 cup flour
½ teaspoon salt
3 tablespoons lard
3 tablespoons water
2 tablespoons butter

Sift the flour and salt. Cut the lard into the flour with a pastry blender until the size of peas. Toss lightly in the bowl and add the water a little at a time. With the finger shape into tiny, ½-inch balls. Brown in the melted butter over low heat, turning frequently. When nicely browned, add to the soup.

MENU:

PENNSYLVANIA DUTCH SOUP WITH DOUGH BALLS
FRUIT SALAD

LA GARBURE

A Basque dish, more of a stew than a soup, is traditional in the southwestern part of France. It is a provincial or simplified version of a pot-au-feu. Any piece of cooked meat and animal fat can be used, although in that part of France goose fat is considered the only one with the proper flavor. It is a robust and variable dish.

½ pound bacon, in 1 piece
2 potatoes, peeled and diced
2 leeks or onions, diced
1 cup peas
1 cup green beans, cut
1 turnip, peeled and diced
2 carrots, scraped and diced
1 red or green bell pepper, cut in strips
½ teaspoon marjoram
¼ teaspoon thyme
2 or 3 cloves garlic
1 small white cabbage, cut in strips, with core discarded
Goose fat, the preserved kind called confit d'oie (*traditional*)
or
1 Italian sweet sausage (*more available*)
Cooked fowl
1 dozen whole roasted chestnuts (*typical but not obligatory*)
Salt and pepper
Wine

Traditionally this is made in a deep earthenware pot that narrows toward the top called a *toupin* but can, of course, be made in any pot that will hold the bulk of this soup. Put the piece of bacon in the pot with 2 quarts of water. Bring to a boil and add the potatoes, leeks or onions, peas, green beans, turnip, carrots, green pepper, marjoram, thyme and garlic. Cook until the vegetables seem half tender. Add the cabbage, a wing or leg of the *confit d'oie* in the unlikely possibility that you have some, or if not, the Italian sausage, a few bacon rinds, pieces of cooked fowl, etc. Cook until it is thick enough to hold up a ladle. Each person adds a little wine to the bouillon as he gets toward the bottom of the soup plate, a custom called *faire chabrot* in southwestern France. *Serves 6 to 8.*

MENU:

LA GARBURE
FRENCH BREAD
AMBROSIA WITH STRAWBERRIES

CREAM OF PUMPKIN AND SHRIMP SOUP

Unlike us, the French do not put their pumpkin in pie, but make soup out of it, among other dishes. It is fine when sufficiently flavored. The pumpkin has a way of blotting out seasonings, so it must be checked by continual tasting. Also, seasonings vary in intensity.

2 pounds pumpkin
1 rib celery, diced
3 cups milk, scalded
2 cups chicken stock
Salt
Freshly ground black pepper
⅓ pound raw shrimp, peeled and cleaned
1 tablespoon lemon juice
⅛ teaspoon nutmeg
Lemon slices
Chopped parsley

Peel the pumpkin and discard the seeds and cottony center. Cut the flesh into small pieces. Place in a heavy saucepan with the celery, milk, stock, salt and pepper. Simmer until the pumpkin is tender, about 30 minutes. Purée the mixture in a blender or put through a food mill or sieve. Return the purée to the pan. Add the shrimp and lemon juice to the purée. Bring to a boil and simmer for

10 minutes. Add the nutmeg. Season to taste with salt and pepper. If too thick, thin with hot milk or stock. It should be the consistency of potato soup. Garnish with lemon slices and chopped parsley. *Serves 6.*

MENU:

CREAM OF PUMPKIN AND SHRIMP SOUP
HOT CLUB ROLLS   BROILED LAMB CHOPS
BAKED POTATOES   CAESAR SALAD
LEMON SHERBET WITH MELON BALLS

WINTER MELON SOUP

This is a dramatic dish fit for a party, especially when cooked and served in the melon. However, some of the Chinese culinary experts dispense with such nonsense. They cut the melon into pieces and cook it in a more straightforward fashion with the other ingredients like a stew. It is much quicker that way, and more in the Chinese manner. The blend of flavors is beguiling and infinitely variable. It can be made with any simple or complex combination of the kind of ingredients that the Chinese use—shrimp, water chestnuts, scallions, green peas, lean ham, etc. A large honeydew melon can be used in place of the winter melon if that is not available.

2 raw chicken breasts, boned, skinned and cut julienne
2 raw thin pork chops, boned and fat discarded, cut julienne
2 thin slices fresh ginger
3 tablespoons dried mushrooms, soaked in warm water
½ cup bamboo shoots, diced
or
2 bunches watercress, chopped
1 small piece cooked Virginia ham, shredded
or
2 pieces Canadian bacon, shredded
1 winter melon (5 to 6 pounds)
Salt and pepper

Put the chicken, pork, ginger, mushrooms and bamboo shoots, if used, in a pot with approximately the right amount of water to fill the melon later. Simmer gently for 40 minutes, then add the ham. Meanwhile cut off the top of the melon and remove the seeds. Pour the mixture into the melon. At this time add the watercress if using that instead of the bamboo shoots. Cover with the melon top. Stand the melon upright in a pot that approximately fits it. Pour water around it about 2 or 3 inches deep. Steam for 1½ hours or until the melon is tender. Present the melon on your best round platter. Ladle the soup into bowls. With a spoon, scoop out some of the melon from the sides of the top for each serving. After 2 or 3 inches have been scooped out, cut that part of the melon off neatly. This is for esthetic reasons. *Serves 4 to 6.*

MENU:

WINTER MELON SOUP
ROAST TURKEY ROLL WITH WALNUT SAUCE
BARLEY AND MUSHROOM CASSEROLE
HOT ROLLS
CHOCOLATE MOUSSE

HAM BONE SOUP

No one in his right mind buys a ham bone just to make soup, but when one gets to the end of a ham it should always be used. Try to leave a little meat on the bone.

1 ham bone with some meat
1 (1-pound, 14-ounce) can tomatoes
1 tablespoon sugar
3 celery ribs, chopped
2 large onions, chopped
½ teaspoon thyme
1 family-size package frozen mixed vegetables
Salt and pepper

Put the ham bone in a soup pot with the tomatoes, sugar, celery, onion, thyme and 3 quarts of water. Bring to a boil and simmer for about 1 hour or more. Remove the ham bone, cut off the pieces of ham clinging to the bone and put them back in the pot. Add the frozen mixed vegetables and cook until barely tender. Add salt and pepper and then serve. This makes a little more than a gallon. What is left over can be frozen. *Serves 16 to 20.*

MENU:

HAM BONE SOUP   CORN MUFFINS
CUSTARD PIE WITH CHOCOLATE TOPPING

DANISH DOUBLE DUMPLING SOUP

Such superb cooks as the Danes and the Pennsylvania Dutch think that two kinds of dumplings in a soup are twice as fine as one. And who's to argue? The meatballs in the Danish soup are a delicate contrast to the sausage ones in the Pennsylvania Dutch soup. Both are excellent.

Meatballs

⅔ cup raw or cooked lean veal or chicken
½ cup dry bread crumbs
½ cup milk
2 tablespoons butter or chicken fat, melted
1 egg white, stiffly beaten
¼ teaspoon salt
Pinch of pepper
Pinch of nutmeg

Chop or grind the meat and pound into a paste. Cook the bread crumbs and milk until they make a paste. Add the butter, beaten egg white and seasonings along with the meat, or purée the meat, bread crumbs and milk in a blender first and then cook until thick. Put through a sieve. Make into 1-inch balls with your hands.

The Dumplings

2 eggs, separated
Milk
1 cup sifted flour
2 tablespoons melted butter or chicken fat
Salt
Pinch of mace
1 tablespoon finely chopped parsley

Put the egg whites in a measuring cup, fill the cup with milk and pour into a pan. Add the flour and butter and blend thoroughly. Stir over low heat until the batter is thick and smooth. Add the egg yolks one at a time, beating thoroughly after each addition. Stir in the salt, mace and parsley.

The Soup

4 cups chicken broth
4 cups beef broth
Finely chopped parsley

Bring the combined broths to a boil. Add the meatballs and simmer for 10 minutes. Two minutes after they have been added to the soup, drop the dumplings by small spoonfuls. Use either a coffee spoon or a half-teaspoon measuring spoon. Then cook for 8 to 10 minutes. Pour in a tureen and serve. Pass more finely chopped parsley to sprinkle on top. *Serves 6 to 8.*

MENU:

DANISH DOUBLE DUMPLING SOUP
FRENCH BREAD
ASSORTED CHEESE
MORE FRENCH BREAD

DRIED FRUIT SOUP

All the ingredients in this soup are things that might be found in any kitchen, but the combination of flavors and seasonings and colors is unusual and most beguiling. The soup is good served either hot or cold and can be kept in the freezer. It is good served just partly thawed on a very hot day.

½ pound chopped beef
1 small onion, minced
¼ teaspoon cinnamon
¼ teaspoon pepper
½ teaspoon salt
½ cup rice
1 small onion, chopped fine
2 tablespoons butter
1 cup dried prunes
1 cup dried apricots
¼ cup chopped walnuts
1 cup chopped parsley
¼ cup canned chick-peas, drained
½ cup vinegar
⅓ cup sugar

Soup Spice

1 tablespoon dried mint
¼ teaspoon cinnamon
¼ teaspoon pepper

Put the meat in a bowl, add the grated onion, cinnamon, pepper and salt. Mix well and roll into small meatballs the size of walnuts. Put 8 cups of water into a 3-quart pot. Add rice and cook for 15 minutes. Meanwhile sauté the chopped onion in the butter and put aside. Add the prunes to the water and rice and cook for 15 minutes more. Add meatballs, apricots, walnuts, parsley, chick-peas and sautéed onions. Cook for about 20 minutes over medium heat. Add the vinegar and sugar. Cook for 15 minutes more. Rub the dried mint in the palm of your hands to make it powdery and release the aroma. Add the cinnamon and pepper to the mint. Sprinkle this in the soup just before removing it from the fire. Check the other seasonings and add more salt and pepper if necessary. *Serves 4 or 5.*

MENU:

DRIED FRUIT SOUP
CHEESE SOUFFLÉ
HOT BISCUITS
COFFEE SHERBET, ITALIAN STYLE
ALMOND MACAROONS

SENATE BEAN SOUP

Once when this soup was not on the menu in the Senate dining room such a fuss was raised that it has not happened again. The soup appeals to legislators and tourists alike, and can be bought for a pittance.

1 pound dried great northern beans
Smoked ham bone with some meat on it
or
Ham hocks
2 onions, chopped
3 tablespoons butter
Salt and pepper

Soak the beans overnight and put on medium heat the next day in the same water in which they were soaked, along with the ham bone or ham hocks. Add more water so that there is about a gallon of beans and all. Cook until the beans are tender and then remove the ham bone or hocks. Sauté the onions in a separate pan in the butter and add to the soup. Season at the end. *Serves 10 to 12.*

MENU:

SENATE BEAN SOUP
BROILED CALVES' LIVER AND BACON
BAKED POTATOES
COOKED GREEN BEAN SALAD WITH VINAIGRETTE DRESSING
ORANGE SHERBET

CORN CHOWDER

A rib-sticking soup that is cheering on a cold gray day.

¼ pound diced salt pork
1 large onion, chopped
½ sweet red or green pepper, chopped
2 large potatoes, peeled and diced
6 soda crackers
3 cups milk
1 (1-pound) can cream-style corn
1 teaspoon salt
½ bay leaf
½ teaspoon thyme
½ teaspoon paprika
Crumbled cooked bacon
Chopped parsley

Sauté the salt pork slowly in a heavy skillet until lightly browned. Add the onion and pepper and cook until onion is golden. Transfer to a deep pan. Add the potatoes and 2 cups of water. Cook until the potatoes are tender and then add the crackers, which have been soaked in milk, and the corn, salt, bay leaf, thyme and paprika. Heat thoroughly. Serve with crumbled cooked bacon and parsley sprinkled on top. *Serves 6.*

MENU:

CORN CHOWDER
MEAT PIROSHKI*
TOMATO AND CUCUMBER SALAD
FRESH PINEAPPLE CHUNKS

GARBANZO SOUP

It's rich and sturdy and easy to make, and, in these days with garbanzos ready-cooked in cans, not even time-consuming. Cooking garbanzos from scratch may be character-building but mostly it's a dreadful nuisance. Unlike that for most other dried beans or lentils, the cooking time varies widely with the age, usually unknown, of the garbanzos. They are not even much more economical when cooked from scratch rather than bought canned.

3 onions, chopped
1 clove garlic, minced
3 tablespoons oil
2 chorizos (Spanish sausages), cut into pieces
1 ham bone
2 bay leaves
½ teaspoon saffron
1 tablespoon Worcestershire sauce
1 large can garbanzos
or
2 (1-pound) cans garbanzos
Lemon juice or vinegar
Salt and pepper

Sauté the onion and garlic in the oil. Put in a deep soup pot with the rest of the ingredients and cover with water. Simmer for 1 hour or longer. It is done when the sausages are tender but the longer it cooks, within reason, the better. Before serving, remove the ham bone and bay leaves, add the lemon juice or vinegar, to taste, for fresh taste and check the seasonings. *Serves 4.*

MENU:

GARBANZO SOUP
GRAPEFRUIT AND AVOCADO SALAD WITH LEMON AND OIL DRESSING
SLICED POUND CAKE WITH CUSTARD SAUCE AND FRESH RASPBERRIES

10

Classic and Sustaining with No Meat

Some of the most beautiful, rich and savory soups in the world are artful concoctions of vegetables, herbs and cheese. There are times, when I have momentarily forgotten the smell of meat cooking, when I think that one could live happily ever after on these. Of course, many have lived without meat and many still do.

LA SOUPE AU PISTOU

A lusty French vegetable soup that is always accompanied by pistou, a near cousin to the Italian pesto, which is stirred in minestrone and so many other soups and dishes. In the South of France the soup is made with fresh white beans and broad beans, but here it can be made with cooked or canned navy or canneloni beans.

La Soupe

1 onion, sliced
3 tablespoons olive oil
2 tomatoes, peeled and chopped
Salt and pepper
Pinch of saffron
½ pound green beans, cut into pieces
or
1 package frozen cut green beans
2 cups cooked or canned navy or canneloni beans
1 medium yellow squash or zucchini, diced but not peeled
½ cup pasta

Pistou

3 cloves garlic
3 tablespoons tomato paste
Leaves from 10 sprigs fresh basil
or
1½ tablespoons fragrant dried basil
¼ cup fruity olive oil
½ cup grated Parmesan cheese

Sauté the onion in the olive oil until slightly colored. Add the tomatoes. When they have cooked down, add 1 quart of water. Season. When the water boils, throw in the green beans, white cooked navy or canneloni beans and squash or zucchini. Cook for about 10 minutes. Then add the pasta. The French use broken pieces, but some of the pretty small shapes are more decorative. In the meanwhile, make the pistou. The French make it in a mortar, pounding the garlic, tomato paste and basil together, then adding the olive oil and Parmesan cheese, little by little, until a saucelike consistency is reached. Some versions omit the tomato paste. When the soup is ready for serving, beat a cup of the broth gradually into the pistou, then pour into the rest of the soup. The pistou can also be made in a blender. Serve with hard-toasted rounds of French bread basted with olive oil. *Serves 6 to 8.*

MENU:

LA SOUPE AU PISTOU
FRENCH BREAD
APPLE PIE

CHESTNUT AND RED CABBAGE SOUP

Cabbage is cabbage, but red cabbage has a slightly different flavor and a most beautiful color. It must be pampered lest it turn into an unappetizing violet. If cooked in an enameled or earthenware pot with a dash of vinegar, all will be well in appearance and flavor. Dried chestnuts from Italian groceries, soaked overnight and then simmered until tender, can be used instead of the fresh.

1 small head red cabbage, shredded
Salt and pepper
2 tablespoons lard
½ cup tarragon vinegar
3 cups beef stock
½ cup red wine
1 pound chestnuts
2 tablespoons sugar
2 tart apples, cored and sliced
⅓ cup currant jelly
½ teaspoon cloves
½ teaspoon caraway seed

Sprinkle the shredded cabbage with salt and pepper. Melt the lard in a large, deep enamel pan. Add the cabbage and sprinkle it with the tarragon vinegar. With a wooden spoon stir the cabbage over low heat for a few minutes. Add the beef stock and red wine. Simmer for a while. Cover the chestnuts with cold water in another pan and boil for 3 minutes. Remove from the fire and drain and rinse with cold water in order to handle them. Peel the outer and inner shells off the chestnuts and add to the soup. Put the sugar in a small pan with 2 tablespoons of water and cook until brown or caramelized. Add to the cabbage and cover. Simmer for about 1½ hours. Add the apples, currant jelly, cloves and caraway seed and simmer for 20 minutes more. Serve in deep bowls. *Serves 4 to 6.*

MENU:

CHESTNUT AND RED CABBAGE SOUP
HOT CORNMEAL MUFFINS
CHOPPED GREEN ONIONS, THIN SLICES OF ORANGE AND FRENCH DRESSING

SOUP BASQUE

Basque food is lusty and sustaining with very little frou frou about it. It is good in a hearty way. Instead of the pumpkin in this recipe, 1 or 2 butterneck squash can be used, depending on the size. A left-over half pumpkin can sometimes be disconcerting if one is not in the mood for pie.

3 tablespoons lard
1 cup chopped onion
1 pound (about) pumpkin
or
Butterneck squash, cut into pieces
1 small white cabbage, cut into pieces
½ pound dried white beans, soaked
2 cloves garlic
Salt and pepper
2 quarts beef stock or water

Brown the onion in the lard, add the squash, cabbage, beans, garlic, salt, pepper and stock or water to cover. Cover and cook for 3 hours over low heat. *Serves 6 to 8 amply.*

MENU:

SOUP BASQUE
COLD BAKED STUFFED TOMATOES
VANILLA ICE CREAM, WITH A SPOON OF STRONG COFFEE POURED OVER EACH SERVING

BROCCOLI AND CHEESE SOUP

A fine and handsome mélange that bears little resemblance to some sad vegetarian dishes.

1 package frozen broccoli
or
1 bunch fresh broccoli, separated and tough bottoms cut off
3 tablespoons butter
3 tablespoons flour
1 quart milk
1 cup grated Cheddar cheese
Salt and pepper

Cook the frozen broccoli in salted water according to directions, or cook the fresh until just tender. Meanwhile, in another pot, melt the butter, add the flour and stir until smooth. Cook for a few minutes. Add some of the milk, a little at a time, stirring constantly until smooth and thickened. Add the cheese and cook over low heat for a few minutes until melted. Add the broccoli and heat thoroughly. *Serves 4 to 6.*

MENU:

BROCCOLI AND CHEESE SOUP
HOT BISCUITS
MIXED GREEN SALAD
APRICOTS

CORN SOUP

One of the less bland of the corn soups.

1 onion, sliced
4 tablespoons butter
2 large tomatoes, peeled, seeded and diced
2 green peppers, seeded and diced
4 cups beef stock
2 tablespoons flour
1 package frozen cut corn
or
1½ cups fresh corn, cut from the cob
Salt and pepper

Sauté the onion in the butter until soft but not brown. Add the tomatoes and peppers and cook with the onion until melted. Pour in the stock and cook for 10 minutes. Sprinkle with the flour and stir until well mixed. Add the corn and continue cooking for about 15 minutes. *Serves 4 to 6.*

MENU:

CORN SOUP
POPPY SEED ROLLS
HAM FETTUCINE
TOSSED GREEN SALAD
PRUNES IN CLARET

RED KIDNEY BEAN SOUP OR POTAGE À LA CONDÉ

There is very little difference, if any, either in flavor or in price, between beans that have been soaked overnight and then simmered until tender and those bought in cans without any sauce. For this recipe buy the canned ones.

2 plump cloves garlic, chopped
2 medium onions, chopped
½ stick (¼ cup) butter, preferably unsalted, melted
2 (1-pound) cans kidney beans, without sauce, drained
2 cups or more beef bouillon
1 cup yoghurt
Watercress

Sauté the garlic and onion in the butter till pale yellow and cooked but not brown. Purée the beans in a blender or put through a food mill. Put in a deep pan with the sautéed garlic, onion, the bouillon and the fat. Heat thoroughly. Serve with the yoghurt and watercress in 2 separate bowls. Let everyone help himself to the embellishments. *Serves 4 to 6.*

MENU:

RED KIDNEY BEAN SOUP
RYE BREAD
ORANGE AND ONION SALAD WITH WATERCRESS AND BLACK WALNUTS

LENTIL SOUP WITH SPINACH

All around the Mediterranean, lentils are cooked with various greens and equally varying flavors. One of the most delicate and different and most difficult of the greens to find in this country is sorrel—called sour grass in the South, where it grows wild. Under different names it can be found growing wild in other regions where the bulldozer has not yet been. It is tedious but rewarding to gather approximately a pound. Lentils can also be cooked with watercress. The soup cooked with sorrel, which has a delicately acid flavor, and the one with watercress, which has a different and spicy flavor, are both puréed and the greens are somewhat indistinguishable except in flavor. In this version, cooked with spinach, the lentils are left whole and the spinach added 15 minutes before serving. It is more colorful than many lentil soups.

2 cups (1 pound) lentils
½ cup sliced onion
¼ cup olive oil
1 tablespoon salt
½ pound fresh spinach, chopped
or
1 package frozen chopped spinach
2 tablespoons lemon juice
4 tablespoons butter (not traditional)

Cook the lentils in 9 cups of water over low heat for 1 hour or until tender. Sauté the sliced onion in the olive oil until golden and add to the lentils. Cook for 1 hour more. Add the washed, chopped (or if frozen, partly thawed) spinach and cook for 15 minutes more. Add the lemon juice and stir. Serve with 1 lump of butter in each bowl. *Serves 4 to 6.*

MENU:

LENTIL AND SPINACH SOUP
POPPY SEED ROLLS
FRUIT SALAD WITH SOUR CREAM DRESSING SPRINKLED WITH POMEGRANATE SEEDS

VIRGINIA PEANUT SOUP

While this is cooked and served in Virginia and Virginians call it their own, it also is found in Bermuda and in different parts of Africa, sometimes with hotter seasoning. It is very rich.

1 small onion, chopped
2 ribs celery, chopped
4 tablespoons butter
2 tablespoons flour
1 cup crunchy peanut butter
4 cups chicken broth (Virginia version)
or
4 cups beef bouillon (African version)
½ teaspoon celery salt
Salt
1 tablespoon lemon juice
4 tablespoons coarsely chopped peanuts

Sauté the onion and celery in the butter until limp and partly melted but not brown. Sprinkle with the flour and stir. Add the peanut butter, stir to blend and add the chicken broth or bouillon, celery salt, salt and lemon juice. Heat thoroughly. Sprinkle the ground peanuts on the top of each bowl before serving. *Serves 4 to 6.*

MENU:

VIRGINIA PEANUT SOUP CHICKEN MARENGO
ESCAROLE SALAD PINEAPPLE SHERBET
NUT KISSES

SOPA DE VERDURAS

This New Mexican version of vegetable soup is quite different from the better-known and more traditional ones. There is an interesting emphasis in its seasoning.

1 beef soupbone with meat
or
6 cups beef bouillon
1 cup green beans
3 small yellow squash, cut into large dice but not peeled
½ onion, chopped
1 red chili pod
1 clove garlic, minced
2 teaspoons salt
1 teaspoon dried mint

Cook the soupbone in 2 quarts of water for 1 hour or longer until reduced to about 6 cups. Strain and discard the bone or use the canned beef bouillon. Add the green beans, squash, onion, chili pod and garlic to the broth. Cook until the beans are tender, about 20 to 30 minutes. Add salt to taste, cautiously if using bouillon. Powder the mint in your hand to release the aroma before sprinkling on top of the soup. *Serves 4 to 6.*

MENU:

SOPA DE VERDURAS
CUBAN BREAD
ORANGE FRITTERS

SPRINGTIME IN THE WINTER SOUP

There comes a day, a gray one, in the winter when spring seems very, very far behind. An inspiriting soup can be assembled from the freezer and things on the shelves that makes one believe again.

½ package frozen asparagus tips or spears
4 cups homemade or canned chicken broth
½ package frozen peas, preferably the petits pois
6 spring onions, with tops and bottoms, chopped
1 buffet can tiny Belgian carrots, drained
or
½ package frozen Belgian carrots
or
3 regular carrots, scraped and slivered
3 tablespoons freshly chopped parsley
Salt, if necessary

Cut the asparagus tips or spears into half-inch pieces. Put in the chicken broth with the peas, chopped onions and Belgian or slivered carrots. Heat until barely tender and still crisp. Sprinkle with the chopped parsley and season if necessary. *Serves 4 to 6.*

MENU:

SPRINGTIME IN THE WINTER SOUP
HOT ROLLS
CHICKEN BREASTS BAKED WITH BUTTER AND TARRAGON VINEGAR
POTATO SOUFFLÉ
LEMON SHERBET WITH STRAWBERRIES
BLACK WALNUT COOKIES

CHEESE SOUP

A lyric, lusty soup to make a Daudet say, *"Oh! la bonne odeur de soupe au fromage!"*

1 cup finely chopped onion
4 tablespoons (½ stick) butter
4 tablespoons flour
2 cups beef bouillon
2 cups freshly grated cheese, preferably Swiss
4 cups milk

Sauté the onion in the butter until limp but not brown. Sprinkle with the flour and continue to cook, stirring well. Add the bouillon a little at a time, stirring until smooth and thickened. Add the cheese and stir until melted. Add the milk, slowly, stirring until blended. *Serves 6 amply.*

MENU:

CHEESE SOUP
FRENCH BREAD
CHEF'S SALAD
CHERRY COBBLER

PEMMICAN

It's true this is neither a dried nor a portable food to sustain one in the barren wilds of the Far North, but emotionally the name seems to suit. It can be made in a simple version or with some embellishments.

1 onion, chopped
2 tablespoons olive oil
1 (7-ounce) package soup mix with mushrooms, sometimes called minestrone vegetables
1 lemon, sliced thin
1 teaspoon turmeric
1 (1-pound) can tomatoes
Salt
Beef base or beef bouillon

For lavish additions

½ pound ground beef
1 package frozen broccoli
or
1 package frozen okra
or
1 package frozen mixed vegetables

Sauté the onion in the olive oil. Add the soup mix with the mushrooms or the minestrone mix or whatever they call it—found in the soup section of the supermarket and usually packaged like a leguminous pousse-café. Add the soup mix to the pot with the lemon, turmeric, tomatoes, salt, beef base with 2 quarts of water or the beef bouillon diluted with some water. The beef does not need to be very strong. Simmer for 30 to 40 minutes or longer, it doesn't matter, but until the dried beans are tender. If you wish the more lavish version, make the ground beef into small balls and add to the soup with one of the frozen green vegetables. *Serves 4 to 6.*

MENU:

PEMMICAN
TOASTED ENGLISH MUFFINS
MIXED GREEN SALAD
PINEAPPLE CHUNKS, APRICOTS AND BLACKBERRIES WITH CRÈME DE CACAO

GUMBO Z'HERBES

This soup is made out of whatever happens to be in the garden, the refrigerator or the market. Any list of ingredients is rather arbitrary. Onions, red pepper and thyme are always there, but not necessarily a carcass of a fowl. Chicken broth or beef bouillon can be substituted for part of the liquid.

1 cup chopped spinach
1 cup chopped green onion, with tops and bottoms
1 bunch watercress, chopped
1 cup shredded cabbage
1 head garden lettuce, shredded
3 tablespoons chopped parsley
Carcass of a chicken, duck or turkey
3 tablespoons bacon fat
1 large onion, chopped
2 tablespoons flour
½ bay leaf
¼ teaspoon thyme
½ pod hot red pepper
1 cup chopped celery
1 tablespoon filé powder
Salt and pepper

Put the first 6 greens to cook in a pot with 2 quarts of water and whatever remnants of cold fowl or game you have at hand. Simmer, covered, for 1 hour and drain. Save the vegetables, fowl and liquor for later use. Sauté the onion in the bacon fat, add the thoroughly drained cooked vegetables and flour and cook over a low heat for 4 minutes. Pour in the liquid in which the greens have boiled. Put the carcass back in the pot and add the rest of the vegetables and herbs. Simmer, covered, for 1 hour. Remove the carcass. Remove the soup from the heat and stir in the filé powder. Season with salt and pepper and serve at once with fluffy rice in a separate bowl. Each puts a spoonful of rice in his bowl. *Serves 6 to 8.*

MENU:

GUMBO Z'HERBES
ROAST BEEF
MASHED POTATOES
VANILLA ICE CREAM
BROWNIES

POTAGE PARMENTIER

Served cold with heavy cream added and sprinkled with chives, this is vichyssoise. It is a starting point for many fine soups such as watercress.

3 to 4 cups (about 1 pound) potatoes, peeled and diced
3 cups (about 1 pound) leeks, including green part, sliced
or
3 cups yellow onions, coarsely chopped
8 cups (2 quarts) chicken stock or water
1 tablespoon salt
¼ to ⅓ cup heavy cream
or
3 tablespoons softened unsalted butter
2 to 3 tablespoons minced parsley or chives

Simmer the vegetables, stock or water and salt, partly covered, for 40 to 50 minutes or until the vegetables are tender. Mash with a potato masher or put through a food mill or purée in a blender. This can be done ahead and the soup refrigerated until needed. Heat, and just before serving remove from the heat and stir in the cream or butter by spoonfuls. Pour into a tureen or individual soup bowls and sprinkle with herbs. *Serves 6 to 8.*

MENU:

POTAGE PARMENTIER
CHICKEN BREASTS, BASTED WITH BUTTER AND VERMOUTH
BARLEY AND MUSHROOM CASSEROLE
WATERCRESS SALAD WITH ROQUEFORT DRESSING
CHOCOLATE MOUSSE

COPAIN'S BLACK BEAN SOUP

Black beans are one of the most beautiful of all the lovely and lusty legumes and often neglected except for the traditional and voluptuously smooth black bean soup. They are exciting and different in this delightful departure from the traditional that is served in the Copain Restaurant in New York City.

2 cups black beans
1 bay leaf
1 ham bone
Pulp of a grapefruit
1 beef bouillon cube
or
1 teaspoon beef-stock base
1 small green pepper, chopped and seeds removed
¼ cup sherry
Cooked rice
1 onion, finely chopped

Soak the beans overnight or for about 8 hours, discarding any that float. Boil with the bay leaf and ham bone until the beans are tender. Add the grapefruit pulp, beef-stock base, chopped green pepper and sherry. Cook ½ hour longer. Serve with a spoonful of cooked rice on one side of the bowl and finely chopped onion on the other. *Serves 6 to 8.*

MENU:

COPAIN'S BLACK BEAN SOUP
ROAST PORK LOIN WITH SPICED CRAB APPLES
SOUBISE
GREEN BEANS WITH ALMONDS
ZABAGLIONE

MUSHROOM AND SOUR CREAM CHOWDER

This can be made with wild mushrooms if you are expert enough to know what you are picking. It is best to go with an expert mycologist. There is no antidote for poisonous mushrooms.

½ pound fresh mushrooms, coarsely chopped
½ cup finely chopped onion
4 tablespoons butter
1 cup diced raw potato
Salt and pepper
Pinch of mace
Pinch of cloves
Dash of Tabasco sauce
¼ teaspoon thyme
2 cups milk
2 egg yolks
¼ cup sherry
2 cups sour cream
Finely chopped parsley
Croutons, cooked in butter

Cook the mushrooms and onion in the butter over low heat for 6 or 7 minutes or until the mushrooms are slightly limp. Stir in the diced raw potato and cook for 12 to 15 minutes more. Season with the salt, pepper, mace, cloves, Tabasco sauce and thyme. Add the milk and bring to a boil. Remove from the fire and add slowly the egg yolks, which have been well beaten with the sherry and sour cream. Return to the fire. Heat but do not boil. Check the seasoning and serve at once in large soup bowls with croutons and sprinkle with the finely chopped parsley. *Serves 4.*

MENU:

MUSHROOM AND SOUR CREAM CHOWDER
BROILED LAMB CHOPS
ITALIAN GREEN BEANS
LETTUCE SALAD
COFFEE CHIFFON PIE

PORTUGUESE KIDNEY BEAN SOUP

A lusty Cape Cod fisherman dish with an unusual, and positive, seasoning emphasis.

1 large can red kidney beans
1 cup diced onion
1 clove garlic, cut in half
2 tablespoons bacon fat
4 medium potatoes, diced
1 can tomato paste
4 or 5 bay leaves
1 teaspoon allspice
Salt and pepper

Put the beans in a deep pan with 4 cups of water. Sauté the onion and garlic in the bacon fat in another pan. Add to the pot, and add the potatoes with the tomato paste, bay leaves, allspice, salt and pepper. Simmer 45 minutes to an hour, adding more liquid if necessary. It should be very thick. *Serves 6 to 8,* but don't count on it. It is the type of soup that one wants several bowls of, so it is not easy to say how many it will serve.

MENU:

PORTUGUESE KIDNEY BEAN SOUP
GRAPEFRUIT AND AVOCADO SALAD
LEMON CHIFFON PIE

POTAGE CRÉCY OR CARROT SOUP

This beautiful buttery golden soup looks as if marigold petals were floating in it but tastes better. It is as good as the carrots with which it is made are young. Older carrots should have the woody center part cut out and discarded. It can be made with chicken or veal stock or with water and still be good. The thickener can be either a diced medium potato or rice as used in this recipe. The rice is a little prettier.

2 cups sliced young carrots
½ cup coarsely chopped onion
1 tablespoon sugar
¼ cup melted butter
1 tablespoon lemon juice
Salt and pepper
½ cup raw rice
4 cups chicken stock or veal stock or water
Very, very finely chopped parsley

Put the carrots in a blender with the onion, sugar, melted butter, lemon juice, salt and pepper until coarsely chopped, stopping the blender and stirring several times with a rubber scraper. Turn into a heavy-bottomed pan. Cook for 15 to 20 minutes or longer until the raw taste is gone from the carrots. Add the rice and chicken stock or veal stock or water. Simmer until rice is tender. *Serves 4 to 6,* depending on the size of the soup bowl you use.

MENU:

POTAGE CRÉCY
RING MOLD OF MEAT LOAF, WITH GREEN BEANS AND MUSHROOMS IN THE CENTER
CHERRY TOMATOES
LEMON SHERBET WITH COINTREAU POURED ON TOP

CLASSIC BLACK BEAN SOUP

This may be the handsomest and most sophisticated of the classic bean soups. The customary garnish is thin slices of lemon and thin slices of hard-cooked eggs, but on an adventurous night drop 7 or 8 fresh white seedless grapes in each bowl. The colors and the flavors are subtle and lovely.

2 cups black beans
2 medium onions, chopped
2 stalks celery, chopped
¼ cup (½ stick) butter
1 ham bone
¼ cup chopped parsley
2 bay leaves
½ teaspoon salt
¼ teaspoon freshly ground black pepper
½ cup dry sherry
2 thin-skinned lemons, sliced thin
2 hard-cooked eggs, sliced thin

Soak the beans overnight and discard any that float. Drain and add 8 cups of cold water. Cover and simmer for about 1½ hours or until tender. The skin will curl back when a few in a spoon are blown upon. Sauté the onion and celery in the butter until opaque but not browned. Add to the beans and cooking liquid with the ham bone, parsley, bay leaves, salt and pepper. Cover and simmer for 3 hours more. Purée the soup in a blender or put through a food mill. Add the sherry and reheat the soup. Serve topped with slices of lemon and slices of hard-cooked egg white for the traditional touch. *Serves 8 to 10.*

MENU:

CLASSIC BLACK BEAN SOUP
BROILED LAMB CHOPS
BROILED TOMATO HALVES
COLD ARTICHOKES
MELON HALVES WITH PINEAPPLE CHUNKS AND STRAWBERRIES

FONDUTA ALLA PIEMONTESE

A reputable Italian cookbook calls this a soup. And what turophile would object to a cheese dish being included in any book under any pretext? The Swiss fondue which is served in many homes and restaurants these days with many flourishes is very very good, but this, I think, is even better. It is made with the Italian fontina cheese, which can be found these days in many fine food departments that carry a selection of cheese. The Italian white truffles are almost as expensive as the French black ones, but not quite. There are some imported from Algiers much less expensive and very enticing.

1 pound imported fontina cheese, diced
Milk
4 tablespoons butter
5 egg yolks
1/8 teaspoon white pepper
4 thick slices toasted French bread, cut into pieces
2 canned white truffles, the size of walnuts, minced fine or sliced paper thin

Place the cheese in a bowl, add enough milk to cover and let stand overnight. Then place the cheese and milk in the top of a double boiler over hot but not boiling water. Beat with an egg beater or stir vigorously with a wooden spoon until the cheese is dissolved. Then stir in the butter, yolks and pepper and cook for another minute or two, stirring constantly. Fonduta should have the consistency of thick cream. Correct the seasoning. To serve put some toasted bread in each bowl. Sprinkle with white truffles and pour in the fonduta. *Serves 4.*

MENU:

FONDUTA ALLA PIEMONTESE FRENCH BREAD
BELGIAN ENDIVE WITH FRENCH DRESSING GLAZED ORANGES

RISI-E-BISI

The risi-e-bisi is nearly always served as a vegetable in America, having been absorbed into our cuisine wholeheartedly without the middle "e." In Italy it is often served in a rather soupy fashion and does indeed make a rather good soup. It is a more substantial meal with crisply fried chicken livers added to it at the last minute.

1 medium onion, finely chopped
1 slice bacon, chopped
½ cup butter
2 tablespoons olive oil
3 to 4 cups hot broth or bouillon
1½ to 2 cups fresh or frozen peas
1½ cups rice
2 tablespoons or more grated Parmesan cheese
Fresh chopped parsley

Sauté the onion and bacon in the butter and olive oil until soft or lightly golden. Add the peas and a cup of the broth, then the rice and more broth. Season with salt and pepper. When the rice is done, serve sprinkled with cheese and dotted with more butter. *Serves 6.*

MENU:

HOT FRIED CHEESE SQUARES RISI-E-BISI
MARINATED ARTICHOKE HEARTS AND SLICED SWEET RED AND GREEN PEPPER
ITALIAN BREAD BROWNIE PUDDING

CREAM OF PIMENTO SOUP

Like many good cream soups, this one has a potato base. The sautéed onion, added at the last, gives an interesting flavor and texture to the soup.

6 medium potatoes, peeled and quartered
½ cup chopped celery
1 teaspoon salt
½ teaspoon pepper
⅛ teaspoon thyme
1 (4-ounce) can or jar whole pimentos, cut into large pieces
2 cups milk
1 cup light cream
1 large onion, finely chopped
2 tablespoons bacon drippings or butter
¼ to ½ cup sherry

Put the potatoes and celery in a deep pot and cover with water. Cook until the vegetables are well done and tender. Drain and reserve the liquid. Mash the potatoes and celery with a potato masher or put through a food mill or purée in a blender. Mix in the salt, pepper, thyme and pimentos. Slowly stir in half the potato water, the milk and the cream. Sauté the onion in the bacon drippings or butter and add to the soup mixture. Heat thoroughly. Just before serving, pour in the sherry. *Serves 4 or 5.*

MENU:

CREAM OF PIMENTO SOUP
COUNTRY CAPTAIN
RICE
SPICED PEACHES
CUCUMBER SALAD

SAUERKRAUT SCHEE

A Russian cabbage soup that is often made with sauerkraut and cabbage. It is almost as well known and loved as the borscht.

- *1 cup chopped onions*
- *2 cloves garlic*
- *3 tablespoons butter or bacon fat*
- *1 (20-ounce) can tomatoes, cut into pieces*
- *2 stalks celery, chopped*
- *2 carrots, chopped*
- *1 small head cabbage, cut into wedges and the core discarded*
- *1 turnip, quartered*
- *4 cups bouillon*
- *1 pound sauerkraut, rinsed and squeezed dry*
- *3 tablespoons lemon juice*
- *3 tablespoons sugar*
- *1 bay leaf*
- *1 tablespoon minced dill*
- *1 tablespoon minced parsley*
- *Sour cream*

Brown the onion and garlic in the butter or bacon fat in a skillet, then transfer to a soup kettle and add the rest of the vegetables and the bouillon. Bring to a boil, simmer for 1½ hours, add the sauerkraut, lemon juice, sugar and bay leaf and simmer for 1 hour more, adding some water if necessary. Check the seasoning. Serve with the minced dill, parsley and sour cream in separate dishes. *Serves 4 to 6.*

MENU:

ROQUEFORT STRUDEL
SAUERKRAUT SCHEE
TOMATO ASPIC WITH WATERCRESS, WHITE GRAPES AND MAYONNAISE
LEMON SPONGE PUDDING

PASTA E FAGIOLI

This is a catchall and infinitely variable Italian bean and pasta soup. Sometimes lentils are used, sometimes cranberry beans or kidney beans or white beans. When there was meat rationing in this country during World War II, Mayor LaGuardia recommended this to harried housewives, calling it in New Yorkese "pasta fazooli."

4 slices bacon, diced
1 medium onion, sliced thin
2 cloves garlic, minced
1 stalk celery, with leaves, chopped
3 or 4 large tomatoes, peeled, chopped and seeded
¼ pound brown lentils (preferably soaked in cold water for 2 hours)
or
1 (1-pound) can kidney beans or ½ pound dried kidney beans soaked overnight
⅓ cup chopped parsley
Salt and pepper
Basil or mint
1 cup tiny pasta (shells, bows, etc.) or broken spaghetti or ditali

Sauté the bacon and set aside. Sauté the onion in the bacon fat and then add the cooked bacon, garlic and celery. Cook for a few minutes and add the tomatoes. Cook about 5 minutes more. Add the drained lentils or kidney beans and stir them around in the fat with the other vegetables. Add the parsley, salt, pepper and basil or mint. Add 2 quarts of hot water. Boil vigorously for about an hour or until the lentils are tender. Add the pasta and cook for 10 minutes more. *Serves 8.*

MENU:

PASTA E FAGIOLI

ITALIAN BREAD

TOSSED GREEN SALAD WITH OIL AND VINEGAR DRESSING

FRESH PINEAPPLE HALVES FILLED WITH FRESH FRUITS AND KIRSCH

CABBAGE AND CARROT SOUP

Simply reeking with color, flavor and vitamins.

2 cans beef bouillon
1 small cabbage, shredded
1 bunch carrots, scraped and cut julienne
½ teaspoon thyme
Salt and pepper, if necessary
Grated Cheddar cheese

Dilute the bouillon with 3 cans of water. Add the cabbage and carrots and simmer uncovered for 45 minutes. The cabbage should be tender and the carrots tender but still crisp. Check the seasoning and serve with the grated cheese sprinkled on top. *Serves 4.*

MENU:

CABBAGE AND CARROT SOUP
HAMBURGERS
POTATO SOUFFLÉ
CHERRY CHEESECAKE

II

Hastily with Love

There is no end to the variety of really fine soups that can be assembled from an imaginative collection of canned and frozen foods and some thises and thats. These are some to trigger further ideas of your own.

TUREEN OF SEAFOOD WITH SAFFRON

A rich and voluptuous dish that can be assembled easily, but not frugally, from a pampered pantry.

1 can lobster, cubed
1 can crab meat, pulled apart
¼ cup (½ stick) butter
½ cup sherry
1 quart half-and-half
1 pinch saffron
1 cup white seedless grapes, fresh or canned

Cook the cubed lobster and crab meat briefly in the butter for flavor. Add the sherry, half-and-half and saffron. Simmer for 15 or 20 minutes but do not let boil. Add the white grapes just before serving. *Serves 4 richly.*

MENU:

TUREEN OF SEAFOOD WITH SAFFRON
HOT BUTTERED TOAST
HEARTS OF BOSTON LETTUCE WITH LEMON AND OIL DRESSING
CHERRY STRUDEL (frozen)

CREAM OF POTATO SOUP WITH GREEN CHILI

It is a personal conviction that Mexican canned green chilies give a hot and pleasing accent to many such bland dishes as this.

2 cans frozen condensed cream of potato soup
4 soup cans milk
1 large can green chili, chopped
½ cup sour cream or yoghurt
Canned pimentos, coarsely chopped

Heat the soup with the milk and green chili. Serve with a blob of sour cream or yoghurt on top. Sprinkle with the pimento. *Serves 4.*

MENU:

CREAM OF POTATO SOUP WITH GREEN CHILI
CANADIAN BACON ROASTED IN 1 PIECE
ZUCCHINI
CORN SOUFFLÉ
GINGERBREAD

CHICKEN BROTH WITH MINCED CLAMS

Inspired simplicity.

2 cans or more clear chicken broth (should total approximately 24 ounces)
1 can minced clams and their juice
2 tablespoons dry French vermouth
Finely minced chives or parsley

Heat the chicken broth with the clams and juice and vermouth. Just before serving, sprinkle the top of each bowl with minced chives or parsley. *Serves 4.*

MENU:

CHICKEN BROTH WITH MINCED CLAMS
LAMB CHOPS
GREEN PEPPER QUICHE
CHERRY TOMATOES
COLD LEMON SOUFFLÉ

CREAM OF CELERY SOUP WITH TINY BELGIAN CARROTS

A no-cooking soup that tastes and looks as if you cared.

1 can condensed cream of celery soup
1 soup can milk
1 buffet-size can Belgian carrots, drained
1 buffet-size can tiny white onions, drained
2 tablespoons slivered raw green pepper

Thoroughly heat the cream of celery soup with the Belgian carrots and tiny white onions. Sprinkle with the slivered green pepper and serve. *Serves 4.*

MENU:

CREAM OF CELERY SOUP WITH TINY BELGIAN CARROTS
HOT BISCUITS
SAUTÉED FLOUNDER
FRENCH-FRIED POTATOES
BOSTON LETTUCE SALAD
BLUEBERRY TURNOVERS

AVOCADO HALVES WITH CURRIED CHICKEN SOUP

Soup served in avocado halves is pleasantly dramatic. The ripe avocado halves are cold and the soup either hot or cold. One spoons down through the soup and brings up some avocado flesh with each mouthful.

1 can condensed cream of chicken soup, diluted with half-and-half or light cream
1 teaspoon or more curry powder
2 ripe avocados, medium to large, cut in halves
Slivered almonds
White grapes
Finely chopped chives

Whether the soup is to be served hot or cold, it is best to heat it first with the curry powder. Then chill, if wished. Serve in the avocado halves sprinkled with the slivered almonds, white grapes and chives. *Serves 4.*

MENU:

AVOCADO HALVES WITH CURRIED CHICKEN SOUP
SESAME SEED BREADSTICKS
DELMONICO STEAKS
RAW SPINACH SALAD WITH HOT BACON DRESSING
COMPOTE OF GREENGAGE PLUMS AND KUMQUATS

CLAM AND ORANGE BROTH

Simple, delicate, delicious and decorative.

1 pint clam juice
1 pint orange juice
Thin slices avocado

Heat the clam juice and orange juice together and serve with thin slices of avocado in each cup or bowl. *Serves 4.*

MENU:

CLAM AND ORANGE BROTH
ROAST BEEF
YORKSHIRE PUDDING
MARINATED HEARTS OF ARTICHOKES
STEWED PEARS IN WINE

CREAM OF PEA AND WATERCRESS SOUP

A fascinating texture and spicy flavor.

2 packages frozen peas
4 tablespoons (½ stick) butter
2 cups chicken broth
½ bunch watercress
1 pint light cream or half-and-half
Salt, if necessary (broth has some)

Cook the peas in the butter for 5 to 10 minutes, then add the chicken broth and half of the watercress. Simmer for 15 to 20 minutes until the peas are tender. Put in a food mill with a course blade. This can be puréed in a blender, but the consistency will be different and not quite as distinctive. Heat with the cream or half-and-half and serve in a tureen sprinkled with the rest of the watercress. *Serves 4 to 6.*

MENU:

CREAM OF PEA AND WATERCRESS SOUP
VEAL SCALLOPINE WITH MARSALA
BROILED STUFFED MUSHROOMS
GREEN PASTA WITH RICOTTA, SWEET BUTTER AND GRATED PARMESAN CHEESE
IRISH COFFEE

TUNA CHOWDER

An easily assembled chowder for two.

1 potato, peeled and diced
1 onion, diced
1 branch celery, diced
2 cups stock
or
1 cup water plus 1 cup milk
1 can tuna, drained
¼ cup hot heavy cream

Simmer the vegetables in the stock or water and milk until half cooked, about 10 minutes. Add the tuna and simmer until the vegetables are cooked but still firm. Serve with 2 tablespoons of the hot cream in each bowl. *Serves 2.*

MENU:
TUNA CHOWDER
PIZZA
FRESH FRUIT

ANCHOVY AND RICE SOUP

A soup that can be easily concocted from ingredients usually on hand, but with an unusual flavor and emphasis.

¼ cup (½ stick) butter
1 onion, minced
⅓ cup raw rice
1 (2-ounce) can anchovy fillets, smashed
3 (10½-ounce) cans beef consommé
3 soup cans water
Grated Parmesan cheese
Anchovies

Melt the butter. Add the onion and cook until limp and pale yellow. Add the rest of the ingredients except for the cheese and whole anchovies. Simmer, covered, for about ½ hour. Serve with freshly grated cheese and a few whole anchovies in each bowl. *Serves 4.*

MENU:

ANCHOVY AND RICE SOUP
RYE ROLLS
TOMATO SALAD WITH VINAIGRETTE DRESSING
HOT GINGERBREAD WITH VANILLA ICE CREAM

CRAB MEAT BISQUE—THE SHORT FORM

One eats this preferably late at night with champagne flowing and possibly some French bread or hot biscuits, but they are not essential—good company is.

1 can crab meat, drained
or
1 package frozen crab meat
1 (10½-ounce) can condensed cream of tomato soup
1 (10½-ounce) can condensed green pea soup
3 cups milk
or
1 pint half-and-half, plus 1 cup light cream
¼ cup bourbon

Pull the crab meat apart and discard any membranes. Put in a pan with the condensed soups and milk or the half-and-half and cream. Either can be used, but the milk is more frugal, less fattening (according to most diets) and less richly sensuous. Cook over low heat until hot enough to serve. Add bourbon, stir well and serve. *Serves 4.*

MENU:

CRAB MEAT BISQUE—THE SHORT FORM
FRENCH BREAD OR HOT BISCUITS
CHAMPAGNE

BLACK BEAN SOUP WITH WHITE GRAPES SERVED IN PINEAPPLE HALVES

The canned condensed black bean soup is one of the best of the canned soups, especially when diluted in equal parts with a beef bouillon. Once when there were unaccountably no lemons in the house, white grapes were used. Since then, it is one of my preferred garnishes. For a truly elegant and impressive presentation, serve the bean soup in pineapple halves. Use the chunks of pineapple that you cut from the halves with peaches in cointreau for the fruit compote at the end of the meal. Obviously, while the soup can be hastily assembled, the preparation of the pineapple is a lengthier process. It can be done ahead.

2 cans condensed black bean soup
Beef bouillon
4 scooped-out pineapple halves
Seedless white grapes
Slivered orange peel

Heat the black bean soup with an equal amount of beef bouillon. Pour into the slightly warmed pineapple halves. Sprinkle with the white grapes and slivered orange peel. *Serves 4.* (This can be served somewhat more simply, of course, in soup bowls—in which case it will serve 4 to 6, depending on what size bowls you use.)

MENU:

BLACK BEAN SOUP WITH WHITE GRAPES, SERVED IN PINEAPPLE HALVES
SESAME SEED BREAD
BROILED CHICKEN BREASTS
BROILED TOMATO HALVES
BOILED TINY NEW POTATOES, IN THEIR SKINS
MIXED GREEN SALAD
BLACKBERRIES AND PINEAPPLE CHUNKS

VALROMEY

An elegant and spendthrift soup that may be assembled easily and quickly, if not frugally.

3 cups strong chicken broth, canned or homemade
¾ cup diced cooked lobster or crab meat
¾ cup canned cooked wild rice
Champagne
Salt and pepper

Heat the chicken broth with the lobster or crab meat and wild rice until boiling. Remove from the fire and add a slug of champagne. Salt and pepper if necessary. *Serves 4 or 5.*

MENU:

VALROMEY
COLD ROAST DUCK
HOT BROILED FRUITS WITH CURRY DRESSING
HOT ROLLS
CHAMPAGNE
LEMON AND MACAROON MOUSSE

GREEN BEAN AND CREAM OF ONION SOUP

There is a picture of this fine combination in the *Encyclopedia of Canadian Cuisine,* but no recipe. So here it is.

2 cans condensed cream of onion soup
2 soup cans milk
1 package frozen Italian green beans or Frenched green beans

Heat the soup and milk together. Meanwhile cook the beans according to the package directions in a separate pan until barely tender but still crisp. Drain and add to the soup just before serving. *Serves 4.*

MENU:

GREEN BEAN AND CREAM OF ONION SOUP
HAMBURGERS
CREAMED POTATOES WITH PEAS (frozen)
GRAPEFRUIT AND AVOCADO SALAD

CREAM OF SHRIMP SOUP WITH BOURBON

Again, even though the soup is to be served cold, it should be heated first. The fine flavor is not quite right when diluted without heating.

2 (10¼-ounce) cans frozen condensed cream of shrimp soup
2⅔ cups milk
1 cup cooked shrimp, fresh or canned
⅓ cup bourbon
Finely chopped fresh dill (nice but not obligatory)

Heat the shrimp soup with the milk to just below the boiling point, stirring frequently. Add the shrimp and chill to serving temperature. Stir in the bourbon. Sprinkle with finely chopped fresh dill, if available. *Serves 6.*

MENU:

CREAM OF SHRIMP SOUP WITH BOURBON
CHICKEN LIVER RISOTTO
SAUTÉED EGGPLANT
MIXED GREEN SALAD
APRICOT CHIFFON PIE

BOULA BOULA

This is one of the most deluxe of the assembled soups. Some versions, not as fine, use the canned pea soup. It is much more delicate with fresh or frozen peas, and suitable for very formal dinners.

3 pounds fresh peas or 2 (10-ounce) packages frozen peas
Salt
1 quart green turtle soup (canned)
⅓ cup good sherry
Freshly ground black pepper
1 cup heavy cream, whipped

Simmer the peas with water and a pinch of salt until tender. Purée in a blender or put through a food mill. Add to the turtle soup. Heat to the boiling point. Add the sherry. Season carefully with salt and freshly ground black pepper. Ladle the soup into 8 individual earthenware or ovenproof china bowls, dividing the turtle meat among them, or put into one large casserole. Cover the tops with the whipped cream. Brown briefly under the broiler. Watch carefully so that the soup does not cool or the cream melt entirely. Serve as soon as the cream browns all over. *Serves 8.*

MENU:

BOULA BOULA
CRÊPES FILLED WITH CREAMED CHICKEN
BROILED TOMATOES
MARINATED HEARTS OF ARTICHOKES
FRESH PEACHES IN RED WINE

QUICK SENEGALESE SOUP

Made either the short way or the long way, this soothes nerves frazzled by nagging heat and lifts one's spirits, too.

4 cups strong chicken broth
1 (4-serving) package instant mashed potatoes
¼ cup apple sauce
2 teaspoons curry powder
1 cup light cream
½ cup diced raw apples
Crumbled cooked bacon

Heat the chicken broth, instant mashed potatoes, apple sauce and curry powder, stirring well. Then chill quickly, if necessary, in the freezer. When ready to serve, stir in the cream. Sprinkle the top with the diced apples and crumbled bacon. *Serves 4 to 6.*

MENU:

QUICK SENEGALESE SOUP
BROILED CHICKEN BREASTS WITH BUTTER AND LEMON JUICE
GREEN BEANS AMANDINE
ROMAINE SALAD WITH FRENCH DRESSING
TANGERINE SHERBET

12
Fruit Soups

These beautiful, delicate and fresh-tasting mélanges of fruit are not easily classifiable. Some start a meal with them, and some serve them for dessert. I rather like them instead of the usual fruit beginning for a leisurely company breakfast.

DRIED FRUIT SOUP WITH CURRY

In Scandinavia, where the winters are very long, fruit soups are often made from habit and necessity with dried fruits. The Scandinavians now have what sounds very funny to Americans—an "instant dried rose hip soup." In the Scandinavian manner, this soup can be served either before the main dish or as a dessert. If serving it as a dessert, try serving it in a tulip champagne glass.

8 ounces mixed dried fruits, with not more than 5 or 6 prunes
3 tablespoons butter
1 tablespoon curry powder
2 cups chicken broth
1 teaspoon grated lemon peel
1 cup sour cream
Chopped crystallized ginger

Soak the fruit overnight. Melt the butter, add the curry powder and cook for a few minutes until blended and the fragrance released. Purée the soaked fruit in a blender or a food mill with some of the liquid, about 1 cup. If this is done in a blender, it should be done in two batches. Put in a soup pan with the chicken broth, lemon peel and butter-and-curry mixture. Simmer for 45 minutes to 1 hour. This can be served hot or cold, depending upon the mood and the temperature outside. Either way, the sour cream is stirred into either the hot or the cold soup just before serving. Sprinkle with the crystallized ginger.
Serves 4 to 6.

MENU:

DRIED FRUIT SOUP WITH CURRY
POT ROAST
POTATO CAKES
MIXED GREEN SALAD

SWEDISH FRUIT SOUP

Serve this instead of the usual fruit for Sunday breakfast. Begin with champagne.

- *2 tablespoons quick-cooking tapioca*
- *2 cups unsweetened pineapple juice*
- *1 tablespoon sugar*
- *½ teaspoon lemon peel*
- *1 (10-ounce) package frozen red raspberries, thawed*
- *½ cup diced orange sections*

Combine the tapioca and 1 cup of the pineapple juice in saucepan and let stand for 5 minutes. Cook and stir over medium heat until mixture comes to a full boil. Remove from heat. Add the sugar, remaining pineapple juice and lemon peel; stir to blend. Cool; then cover and chill. Before serving, fold in the raspberries and orange sections. *Makes 3½ cups or 4 servings.*

MENU:

SWEDISH FRUIT SOUP
SEAFOOD QUICHE
CROISSANTS
ESPRESSO

WINE SOUP

Joan of Arc is said to have been nourished by wine soup during the siege of Orleans. It was probably not one like this, which is best served ice-cold in the Scandinavian way as a dessert.

- *2 cups dry white wine*
- *1 tablespoon sugar*
- *1 piece lemon peel*
- *1 piece cinnamon stick or pinch of ground cinnamon*
- *1 tablespoon cornstarch*
- *2 egg yolks, lightly beaten*

Bring the wine and 2 cups of water to a boil with the sugar, lemon peel and cinnamon. Mix the cornstarch with a little water and add to the wine mixture. Cook, stirring with a wire whisk, until slightly thickened, about 5 minutes. Stir a little of the hot mixture into the egg yolks and then beat into the rest of the wine mixture. Chill thoroughly. Serve in well-chilled cups or bowls with 2 fresh Bing cherries with stems in each bowl and some madelines on the side. *Serves 5 or 6.*

MENU:

BROILED CHICKEN
POTATO SALAD
HOT BISCUITS
WINE SOUP
MADELINES

MINNA'S LEMON SOUP

A perfect soup for, say, after Thanksgiving dinner when you think you want something but not really. It is also a light, fresh preamble to a meal, or being a Danish soup can be served as the Danes serve it—at the end of a meal for dessert with thin almond cookies.

3 tablespoons butter
3 tablespoons flour
Grated peel of 1 large or 2 small lemons
Juice of 1 large lemon or 2 small lemons
3 egg yolks, well beaten
3 tablespoons sugar

Meringue

2 egg whites
2 tablespoons sugar
Cinnamon

Melt the butter and blend in the flour. Cook together for a few minutes and then add 1 quart of water a little at a time, stirring until smooth and thickened. Add the grated lemon peel and boil for about 10 minutes. Remove from the stove. Add the lemon juice to the soup, then add a ladle of the soup to the well-beaten egg yolks and sugar. Return to the mixture, which is still off the stove. Stir until smooth and pour into soup bowls. Beat the egg whites stiffly, adding the sugar gradually. Put a spoonful in each soup bowl, sprinkled with the powdered cinnamon. This can be served either hot or well chilled. *Serves 4 or 5.*

MENU:

PORK CASSEROLE WITH SOUR CHERRIES, GREEN PEPPER AND RICE
MINNA'S LEMON SOUP
THIN ALMOND COOKIES

STRAWBERRY SOUP

Serve the soup last in the Scandinavian fashion with thin crisp cookies.

2 (10-ounce) packages frozen strawberry halves, partially thawed
¼ cup sugar
2½ tablespoons quick-cooking tapioca
Dash of salt
1 tablespoon lemon juice
½ cup grapefruit and orange sections (nice but not obligatory)

Press strawberries through a sieve or ricer or blend until smooth in a blender. Place the puréed fruit in a saucepan. Add 2 cups water and the sugar, tapioca and salt. Let stand for 5 minutes; then cook and stir over medium heat until mixture comes to a full boil. Remove from heat and add lemon juice. Cool, stirring after 15 minutes. Chill. Add grapefruit and orange sections just before serving. *Serves 4.*

MENU:

CURRIED CHICKEN
RICE
CHUTNEY
COLD ARTICHOKES WITH FRENCH DRESSING
STRAWBERRY SOUP
THIN ALMOND COOKIES

COLD CHERRY SOUP

In Scandinavian countries and Germany, cherries are more apt to appear in soup than in pie. On a day almost too hot to bear, serve the soup ice-cold to start the meal in the German manner or as a liquid dessert in the Scandinavian way.

1½ pounds pitted sweet or sour cherries
1 cup red wine
¼ to ½ cup sugar or more, according to cherries and taste
½ teaspoon grated orange peel
1½ teaspoons arrowroot
Whipped cream or tiny macaroons

Put the cherries, red wine, 3 cups of water, sugar and orange peel in an enameled pan. Cook over medium heat until soft, about 10 minutes. Purée in a blender or put through a sieve. Thicken the soup with arrowroot mixed with a little of the cooled juice. Add more sugar if necessary. Cook for a minute or two until thickened and clear. Chill. Serve with a dollop of whipped cream on each bowl or macaroons in the bottom. *Serves 6.*

MENU:

SALAD NIÇOISE (tuna fish, cooked green beans, black olives, tomatoes, hard-cooked eggs, etc., with French dressing)

HOT BISCUITS

COLD CHERRY SOUP

13

Garnish and Adorn

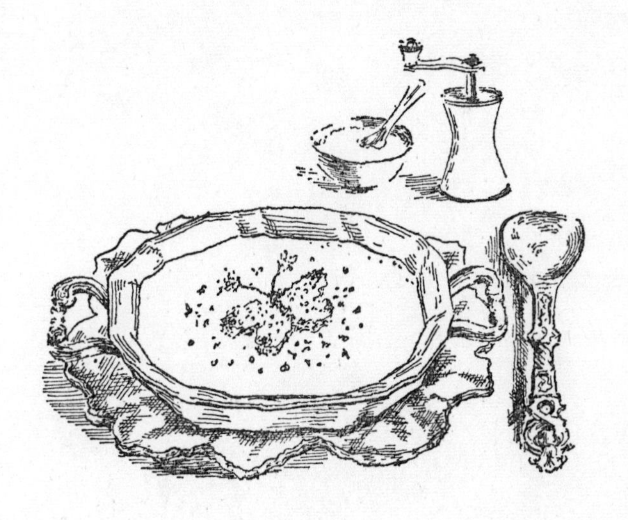

The art of garnishing a soup can be a delight but can also be a trap for the unwary. Too many garnishes or a too ambitious and pretentious garnish can be a visual and gastronomic disaster. A garnish can be as simple and lovely and inexpensive as a frill of parsley on a pale green cream of asparagus soup, or one charming pimento star floating on a cream of chicken soup. It can also be a rich, savory and wondrously odorous concoction called pesto,* which can be prepared ahead of time to enhance a bowl of minestrone, for which it was created by some ancient genius; or it can be small spoon-shaped, voluptuous and velvety quenelles, which may be made of chicken, veal or fish, whichever is available and compatible with the soup.

All kinds of breads and dumplings are in natural harmony with soup, whether served in the soup, like all the many large and small dumplings, or served on the side as is the habit in many countries. The Russians serve their pirogi or piroshki on the side sometimes, other times preceding the soup and now and then as a separate course following the soup. Sometimes there are several different fillings in one large pirog or kulebiaka, which is made in a large rectangle and cut into pieces to serve.

Which of the many garnishes is served with each soup is a matter of individual taste, local availability, mood and occasion. The Japanese can make a soup, apparently of no substance all with a delicate, elusive taste, look elegant and distinctive by floating a few thin slices of raw vegetables cut into entrancing shapes. At the stores with fancy food and cooking equipment, there are round boxes of small cutters called French vegetable cutters that will do this. They sell, even in this inflated age, for what might be called a pittance.

Some of these fresh and crisp and simple garnishes are handsome enough without much tampering. Watercress, fresh dill, chervil, chives, fresh mint or parsley, finely chopped and sprinkled on top, gives a soup a lovely look and a fresh good taste. Freshly grated cheese, crumbled cooked bacon, grated coconut and slivered almonds or almost any of the coarsely chopped nuts add a nice touch.

Any freshly cooked vegetable, cut into small neat pieces—asparagus, thin-sliced zucchini or yellow squash, small flowerets of broccoli or baby okra—adds its bit in color and good taste. Raw mushrooms, sliced lengthwise through the cap and the stem, thin crisp slices of water chestnuts, red onion rings and small pieces of crystallized ginger zip up some soups—but please, not at the same time. The mushrooms or the water chestnuts are more decorative when used in a soup with some color contrast, say a cream of tomato or cream of asparagus.

Thin slices or pieces of fruit—oranges or lemons, cherries, white grapes, pineapple chunks or kumquats—are fresh and decorative in many soups. As an attention-getting device, strew pomegranate seeds on top of an otherwise bland and pale cream soup.

Whipped cream or sour cream, plain or flavored with curry, ginger, horseradish or paprika, is good with almost all of the soups that begin a meal. Quartered or sliced hard-cooked eggs and small pretty shapes of pasta look handsome in clear soups and give them a pleasing textural contrast. Some European cookbooks suggest poached pigeon eggs, which would indeed be a dainty touch. Unfortunately, although most of the cities I have lived in are overinhabited by pigeons, no one but the pigeons seems to know or care what happens to the eggs.

Throughout this book are recipes for rouille sauce,* pesto,* aioli,* many kinds of meatballs, stuffed eggs, quenelles and royal custard with green chili. For the classically simple royal, omit the pepper. Roman frozen ravioli, available in the frozen foods department of supermarkets, can be cooked in a soup instead of making your own capelleti or won ton. The quenelles, delicate mousses of chicken, veal or fish, can be made simply in a blender, and Scandinavian fish balls in cans can be used to give a delicate distinction to many soups. Thin strips of omelet give a sophisticated touch: Beat 1 whole egg with 2 tablespoons of flour and ½ cup of liquid—milk, consommé, bouillon or fish broth—and ½ teaspoon of chopped chervil, parsley or chives. Fry like a pancake and cut in thin strips.

All kinds of dumplings from the very large to the very small are a gastronomic adornment to soups. They can be made from scratch or from a biscuit or corn-bread mix and added by the spoonful to the soup either as is or with a few little bits of watercress, bacon, finely chopped onion or ground ham stirred in.

Cranberries can be added to the dumplings for hot wine soup. Do this as the spirit moves and the soup demands.

Tiny unsweetened cream puffs called profiteroles are amazingly simple to make, but impressive to see floating in a clear broth or consommé. Thick slices of French bread cut on the bias and toasted, then sprinkled profusely with clouds of freshly grated cheese, are classic in many French and Italian soups and good in many others. Pilot biscuits, the real kind, sometimes called captain's biscuits or sea biscuits or hardtack, are about 3 inches in diameter, almost an inch thick and hard like bagels, to use a symbol familiar to New Yorkers. Split them in half and soak in water for about 10 minutes. Remove them with a spatula, put on a cookie sheet with a dab of butter on each and heat in a very hot oven for 20 minutes, watching carefully so they don't burn. They are served very very hot, are indigenous to New England, but are enjoyed wherever they are known. The refrigerated biscuits in tubes in the supermarkets can be filled with egg salad, sautéed chicken livers, mushrooms or Smithfield ham spread. Put a spoonful on each, fold over into half circles and bake according to directions. Serve as Americanized piroshki.

Butter Dumplings

2 tablespoons butter
2 eggs
6 tablespoons flour
¼ teaspoon salt

Cream the butter until soft. Then add the eggs and beat in. Stir in the flour and salt. Drop the batter from a spoon into simmering soup and simmer the dumplings covered for about 8 minutes. *Makes about ¾ cup batter.*

Matzo Balls

3 eggs, separated
¾ cup matzo meal
½ teaspoon salt
¼ teaspoon pepper

Beat egg yolks until light and fold in the matzo meal, salt and pepper. Fold in stiffly beaten egg whites and let the mixture stand 5 minutes. Drop by teaspoon in boiling soup. Cook for 45 minutes in tightly covered pot. *Makes 12 balls.*

Cheese Dumplings

3 tablespoons butter
½ cup grated Swiss cheese
2 tablespoons flour
1 egg yolk
1 tablespoon minced parsley
Salt and pepper

Cream the butter and cheese in a warm bowl and add the flour, egg yolk, parsley, salt and pepper. Form the dough with your fingers into small dumplings about 1½ inches in diameter. Drop them into the gently boiling soup. Continue boiling until the dumplings rise to the surface. Serve at once. *For a small soup for 4, to precede a meal.*

Profiteroles

1 cup milk
⅓ cup butter
1 cup sifted flour
Pinch of salt
4 eggs, at room temperature

Put the milk and butter in a heavy pan and bring to a boil. Add the flour all at once and stir quickly with a wooden spoon until smooth and the sides of the pan are left clean. Remove from the heat and let cool for about 2 minutes. Add the eggs, one by one, beating well after each addition. When all the eggs are done and the paste no longer looks slippery, drop by ½ teaspoons or put through a pastry bag with a ½-inch tip on a greased baking sheet. Bake in a preheated 400° oven for about 10 minutes. Add to the soup just before serving. *Makes 1½ cups of batter.* The number of puffs depends on the size.

SALMON PIROG

Pastry

½ cup (1 stick) butter
4 ounces cream cheese
1 cup sifted flour

The Filling

¼ cup finely chopped shallots
1 clove garlic, minced
½ stick butter
½ pound mushrooms, sliced
2 tablespoons chopped fresh dill
or
1 teaspoon dill weed
½ cup fish stock (liquid from cooking salmon)
1 teaspoon salt
¼ teaspoon freshly ground black pepper
Dash of nutmeg
2 fresh salmon steaks, about 1 inch thick, cooked, skinned, boned and cut into large pieces
2 cups cooked cold rice
3 hard-cooked eggs, chopped
Salt and pepper to taste
1 egg yolk, lightly beaten

Preheat the oven to 400°. Sauté the shallots and garlic in the butter until tender. Add the mushrooms and dill and cook 3 to 5 minutes. Add fish stock, the 1 teaspoon of salt, pepper and nutmeg and bring the mixture to a boil. The consistency should be mushy. Mix the mushroom mixture with the salmon chunks and cool to room temperature. For the pastry, cream the butter and cheese until well blended. Add the flour and mix until smooth. Roll out the dough on a lightly floured pastry cloth into a rectangle at least 12 by 8 inches. Spread 1 cup of the rice in the middle of the dough, leaving at least 2 inches on all sides clear. Spread half of the fish mixture on top of the rice, cover with the chopped eggs and season to taste with salt and pepper. Pile the remaining fish and then the remaining rice on top of the eggs, making a meat-loaf shape. Draw the long edges of the dough together over the filling and pinch to seal. Cut off a triangle from each corner and then fold the ends, like envelope flaps, up over the covered filling and seal. Place on a lightly greased and floured baking sheet face down on the sealed edges, so that the smooth dough is on top. Brush the pirog with the egg yolk mixed with 2 tablespoons of water. Make 2 or 3 steam holes in the top and bake for 15 minutes or until brown. Reduce heat to 350° and cook 15 minutes longer, or until the bottom dough is cooked. *Serves 6 to 8.*

PIROSHKI

The Dough

1 package yeast
¼ cup lukewarm water
1 cup milk
3½ cups sifted flour (approximately)
2 eggs
1 tablespoon sugar
1 teaspoon salt
2 tablespoons melted butter

Soften the yeast in the water. Bring the milk to a boil and cool to lukewarm. Add the softened yeast. Add about half the flour and beat until smooth. Cover and let stand until light, 30 minutes or longer. Blend 1 egg yolk with 1 tablespoon water, cover and set aside. Mix the remaining egg white and whole egg, sugar, salt and melted butter. Add to the yeast mixture and blend. Add enough of the remaining flour to make a fairly soft dough. Knead until dough is smooth and elastic, about 8 to 10 minutes. Turn into a greased bowl, grease the top, cover with a towel and let rise in a warm place (80 to 85°) until doubled in bulk, about 1½ hours. Squeeze off small egg-sized pieces of the dough and shape into balls. Roll each to less than ¼-inch thickness on a floured board. Place a rounded teaspoon of meat filling (see below) in the center, fold the sides of the dough over the filling and roll into a long shape with tapering ends and a plump center. Place on a greased baking sheet, cover and let stand until the dough is light, about 20 minutes. Brush the tops with the reserved egg-yolk mixture and bake in a preheated oven at 425° for 15 minutes. Lower the oven temperature to 400° and bake until brown, about 20 minutes longer.

Meat Filling

6 tablespoons butter
½ pound lean beef, ground
¾ cup water or meat broth
2 medium onions, chopped
2 tablespoons flour
1 teaspoon salt
Freshly ground black pepper to taste
2 tablespoons chopped parsley
or
¼ teaspoon powdered dill

In a skillet heat half the butter, add the meat and cook until brown. Remove the meat from the pan and grind again, using the finest blade of a food grinder. Add the liquid to the skillet and heat while scraping loose the browned particles. In a separate skillet heat the remaining butter, add the onion and cook until brown. Stir in the flour. Add the liquid from the first skillet and cook, stirring, until thickened. Mix all the ingredients and season to taste.

14
Basics

These are the basics of fine soup (sauce) making that all chefs have on hand, as do and should the gifted and serious home cooks.

WHITE VEAL STOCK

This is not used as frequently and ubiquitously as beef or chicken stock, but it is good to have on hand for some dishes.

2 pounds veal bones, chopped into small pieces by the butcher
1 pound veal, cut into chunks
2 onions, sliced
2 leeks, sliced
2 carrots, sliced
1 small turnip, peeled and diced
3 stalks celery, diced
Pinch of thyme
½ bay leaf
2 peppercorns
2 cloves
1 teaspoon salt

Put the veal bones in boiling water for 3 minutes. Rinse in cold water and put in a pan with the other ingredients and 2 quarts of water. Simmer for 2 hours. Strain, chill and remove the fat. This can be packaged in small containers and frozen. *Makes 5 or 6 cups.*

GLACE DE VIANDE

One must have a serious approach to cooking to make this. It is not just that it takes a lot of time, but sometimes there is a psychic shock at the idea of cooking 4 pounds of beef and assorted vegetables until they are reduced to ½ cup of concentrated essence of beef. Yet a cube or two of this paste can make a dish truly distinguished.

Make the beef stock according to the recipe (see Index), using 4 pounds of beef. Instead of simmering for 5 hours, simmer it for 6 to 7 hours. Strain and chill. Remove the fat from the top and any speck of meat or vegetable. Reheat and strain through double thicknesses of cheesecloth into a shallow pan. Simmer until this is reduced to half its quantity. Chill again and remove any bit of fat that still lingers. Put in a small pan set in a larger pan of water and cook until further reduced to about ½ cup or slightly more. Put in a bowl and chill. Then dice and let dry out before packaging. One or two cubes are put into a gravy, sauce or soup, while it is being made, for a professional finish and an exquisite flavor.

FISH FUMET

Unlike beef or chicken stock, the fish takes very brief cooking—about ½ hour, and is simply wonderful to have on hand for fish soups or sauces. With everything packaged these days, one has to look for a fish man with a supply of fish heads and bones. Again, freshly caught fish are best. The fumet can be frozen and kept on hand.

2 pounds assorted white fish cut into pieces
1 pound fish heads and bones
1 cup white wine
2 leeks, sliced
1 onion, sliced
1 stalk or branch of celery, chopped
6 sprigs parsley
½ bay leaf
¼ teaspoon thyme
1 clove
1 teaspoon salt
White pepper

Put all the ingredients in a pan with 6 cups of water. Simmer for ½ hour. Then strain, cool and freeze. If frozen in a regular ice-cube tray, the cubes can then be removed and packaged in a Pliofilm bag in the freezer. In this way, a little can be used at a time. *Makes about 5 or 6 cups.*

BEEF STOCK

So many soups, so many sauces and so many dishes are made with beef stock that a perfectly made one can make the difference between a superb dish and a mediocre one. It is something that one can be long and blissful in the doing.

3 pounds beef and/or veal knucklebones
3 pounds stewing beef, cut into chunks
2 pounds beef shank with bone, meat and marrow
1 onion, quartered but not peeled
1 clove garlic, halved
1 leek, halved
2 stalks celery with leaves
1 carrot, quartered lengthwise
1 parsnip, quartered lengthwise
1 lemon, sliced
or
½ teaspoon citric crystals
½ teaspoon mixed pickling spices

Place all the meat and bones in a large kettle with 3 quarts of water. Bring to a rolling boil and then reduce the heat. Remove the gray scum from the top of the kettle. This will not affect the flavor of the soup if left in, but the stock will not be as clear. Continue skimming until there is no more foam. Add the vegetables, lemon or citric crystals and seasonings. Cover and simmer for 4 or 5 hours. Strain through a sieve lined with several thicknesses of cheesecloth into a large bowl. When slightly cooled, refrigerate uncovered. After several hours or preferably overnight remove the fat and package some of the clear stock and some of the stock with the chunks of beef into pint plastic freezing containers, to be kept frozen until needed. The stock will keep in the refrigerator with the fat left on as a protective topping for a week to 10 days without freezing. The fat when removed can be used in gravy or sauces. This makes about 3 quarts, but the exact amount depends a lot upon how long the bouillon is simmered. The longer it cooks, the more concentrated it becomes.

INDEX